Table of Contents

Vegetable Salsas

Fruit Salsas

Guacamole

I would like to dedicate this book to my beautiful wife, Michelle Lynn, my daughters Taylor, Madison and Paige and my son, Chase. I would also like to thank the real genius behind this book, Jennifer Dean, for her shared commitment to high quality, healthy foods. Last but not least, I would like to thank my salsa mentor, my father-in-law, Jerry Rodger Jones, for introducing me to homemade salsa over a decade ago.

Also, a special thanks to our text editor, Pam Perry.

We would also like to thank the following Associations:

California Avocado Commission

National Onion Association

California Tomato Growers Association

Salsa & Guacamole

The Secrets to Their Success

While salsa and guacamole used to be a well-kept secret of the south, they are now consumed and enjoyed worldwide, with a dizzying array of tasteful variations. Fresh fruits and vegetables, herbs and spices all mix and mingle to create tastes that dance across the tongue with delightful, if sometimes eye-watering results. While there are many variations to the traditional salsa and guacamole recipes of old, the main staples remain the same: tomatoes, onions and avocados. This trio creates a colorful and appetizing combination and packs a healthy punch most consumers are unaware of.

Lycopene gives tomatoes their red color and, research says, has countless healthy benefits. Many recent epidemiological studies have linked lycopene to the prevention of cancer and cardiovascular disease. Other studies have also linked lycopene to an enhanced immune system. More than 80 percent of the lycopene consumed in the United States is derived from tomato products.

The sulfur-containing compounds responsible for an onion's pungent odor are also the reason for their many health benefits. It has been found that consumption of onions has a lowering effect on blood sugar levels; the higher the onion intake, the lower the level of glucose found in testing. Chromium, a mineral found in onions, helps cells respond to insulin. A regular ingestion of onions has also been found to lower cholesterol and high blood pressure, both of which help prevent atherosclerosis and diabetic heart disease and reduce the risk of heart attack or stroke. Studies have also linked onion consumption to a lowered risk of colon cancer and have found that they help maintain healthy bones.

Avocados are a rich source of mono unsaturated fatty acids which have been shown to offer significant protection against breast cancer and to lower cholesterol levels. They are also a good source of potassium, a mineral that regulates blood pressure. Potassium helps guard against heart disease, high blood pressure and stroke. They are also a great source of folate, a nutrient important for heart health. Avocados contain the highest amount of carotenoid lutein of all commonly eaten fruits. Carotenoids are lipid (fat) soluble so the fat in avocados is a necessity nature saw fit to incorporate so these bioactive carotenoids could be easily dissolved into the blood stream. Mixing avocados into a fresh salad or adding some chopped avocado to your fresh salsa will increase your body's ability to absorb the health-promoting carotenoids that vegetables provide.

Epidemiological studies - a type of study in which the diet consumed by individuals is compared to their development of diseases over a period of years or decades - have shown that people who consume fresh fruits and vegetables have a lowered risk of many types of cancers and chronic diseases, have healthier aging processes and higher energy levels. The consumptions of higher amounts of fresh fruits and vegetables has been linked specifically to lowered risks of cardiovascular-vascular disease, asthma, chronic bronchitis and arthritis.

Childhood obesity is becoming an epidemic in the United States. Research estimates that about 22 percent of children today are considered obese. A diet that includes fresh fruits and vegetables is essential to healthy growth and development. The habit of healthy eating can be learned from home and carried to adulthood. Many of the recipes in Viva Salsa can be fun and simple family cooking adventures. From tropical fruits to crisp vegetables or savory legumes, the compilation of recipes in the Viva Salsa cookbook and also on the Viva Tortilla Web site, www.vivatortilla.com, appeal to any palate, from the most modest of taste buds to the most discerning.

The Tomato

Tomatoes first grew as wild, cherry-sized berries in South America. Mexico developed the now familiar tomato, known then as tomatil. The tomatil traveled to Europe with the conquistadors and was taken to Italy. Italians considered it an aphrodisiac and gave it the Italian name poma amoris, meaning "love apple."

By nature the tomato is defined as a fruit because it is the ripened ovary of a plant, but in 1893 the U.S. Supreme Court declared that tomatoes were vegetables. Today they are classified as a vegetable. California is the world's largest producer of processed tomatoes, accounting for nearly half the world's production. Florida is the world's largest fresh tomato industry.

Tomatoes are packed with a surprising number of vitamins and nutrients. One four-ounce tomato contains about one-third of the recommended daily allowance for vitamin C, plus a little beta carotene, potassium, folic acid and other B vitamins, iron and fiber. Lycopene, a potent antioxidant, is the agent that gives a tomato its red color and has been found to prevent cancer.

The Onion

Onions have a long and flavorful history. There is documentation that onions grew in Chinese gardens as far back as 5000 years ago. Egyptians can trace their use back to 3500 B.C. and Sumerians were growing onions as early as 2500 B.C.

It is thought that the onion dates back so far because it is so much less perishable than many other foods of the time. It was also easy to grow because it thrives in a variety of soils and climates.

By the middle ages, the three main foods consumed by most Europeans were beans, cabbage and onions. Onions were also being used for their medicinal qualities as a cure for headaches, snake bites and hair loss.

The first pilgrims brought onions to the Americas, but found that many varieties of wild onions already grew throughout North America.

At least 175 countries grow onions. According to the United Nations Food and Agriculture Organization, there are an estimated 6.7 million acres of onions in the world. About 105 billion pounds of onions are produced each year. The National Onion Association estimates there are about 1,000 onion growers in the United States with 145,000 acres of onions planted in the United States annually.

The Chile Pepper

A staple of any delicious Mexican fare is the chile pepper. Despite their spicy reputation, the chile pepper comes in a wide variety of tongue-tickling colors and tastes. The heat of a chile pepper is concentrated in the interior vein. A colorful indication that a chile pepper is of the spicier variety is a yellowish-orange shading in that vein.

In 1912 a pharmacist named Scoville created a heat index for chile peppers, appropriately named "Scoville Units." Today this measurement is called the "Official Chili Pepper Heat Scale" and carries a rating scale of zero to 10, with 10 being the most potent.

More than 140 varieties of chile peppers are grown in Mexico alone. Here are a few of the most popular chilies in the United States:

Bell Peppers

The tasty trio of red, green and yellow bell peppers is probably the most commonly used pepper. These rate on the low end of the Official Chili Pepper Heat Scale with a mild, sweet taste.

Ancho Peppers

Look and taste a lot like bell peppers but can be considerably more peppery in flavor. They turn bright red and get much sweeter in taste in the fall.

California Green Chilies

Otherwise known as Anaheim Peppers, these peppers can pack a punch with a wide range of flavors from mild and sweet to moderately hot. Check the vein for coloring to decipher heat scale.

Chipotle Chilies

These are made from jalapeños that have been dried and smoked.

Salsa
and
Guacamole

The World's Best
Salsa and Guacamole Cookbook

Nicholas Webb

Edited by Jennifer Dean

Published by
Lassen Scientific, Inc.

Viva Tortilla is a Trademark of Lassen Scientific, Inc.

ISBN: 1-59971-176-1

For more information visit

Lassen Scientific, Inc.
www.lassenscientific.com
www.vivatortilla.com

Jalapeño Chili Peppers

These are hot! Canned and bottled peppers are sometimes labeled "hot peppers," with jalapeño as a subtitle.

Poblano Chilies

These are dark green, similar in size to a bell pepper but tapered at one end. They can be mild or hot. They are often used in "chile rellenos."

Serrano Chilies

Small, fresh HOT peppers. The smaller in size, the hotter the pepper. They are most often used in Pico de Gallo.

Yellow Chile Peppers

Many short, conical-shaped yellow peppers go by this name. Some examples are: Santa Fe grande, caribe, banana peppers, Hungarian, Armenian way, floral gem and gold spike. Flavors range from medium/hot to hot.

Habanero Peppers

These are the hottest peppers known to man. They are marble-shaped chile peppers that range in color from an unripe green to full ripe red.

To dry chile peppers tie stems to a sturdy piece of twine and hang in dry area with good air circulation. In several weeks chilies lose their brilliant hue, changing to deep red. They will feel smooth and dry.

Chili Pepper Tips:

Always wear gloves when touching chilies, especially the hot ones!

- Do not touch your face or eyes after touching a chile pepper.
- Cutting out the vein center of a chile will lessen its heat.
- Removing the seeds from a chile will also lessen its heat.

Vegetable Salsas

Hot

Smoked Habanero Salsa

5 whole habaneros, seeded
10 whole tomatillos, husked and rinsed
2 whole Vidalia onions
1 red onion, chopped
6 whole sweet red peppers, seeded
2 whole smoked habaneros
3 whole chipotle peppers
1 Tbl cumin
2 oz balsamic vinegar
1/2 c fresh cilantro, chopped

Process ingredients in a blender individually in order listed until you reach the dried peppers and place in a non-reactive container. Place smoked habaneros and chipotles in blender and drain juice from mixture in bowl into the blender and process. Add to the mixture in the bowl. Add cumin and cilantro and stir well. Drizzle balsamic vinegar over the top. Let marinate overnight.

Anaheim Red Onion Salsa

4 large fresh ripe red tomatoes
4 fresh green Anaheim chilies
1 red onion, chopped
1 clove garlic, chopped finely
1 Tbl salt
2 Tbl lime juice

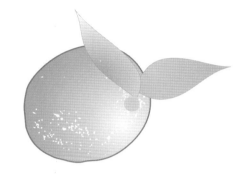

Roast the tomatoes and green chilies on
a gas grill or under the oven broiler until
charred and blackened.
Place the blackened chilies in a Ziploc
freezer bag and let steam for about 10 minutes.
Meanwhile, remove the skin from the tomatoes, cut them in half and remove the seeds.
Then chop them into squares about 1/2 inch in size.
Remove the chilies from the plastic bag and chop them. Combine with tomatoes and
add the onion, garlic, salt, lime juice, olive oil and cilantro. Black pepper to taste. Add
sprig of oregano and let chill for about an hour.

Canned Salsa

4 jalapeño peppers
3 cloves garlic, chopped finely
1 white onion, chopped finely
1/2 red onion, chopped finely
1 Tbl white sugar
1 tsp salt
1/4 tsp ground cumin
1 lime, juiced
1 (10oz) can diced tomatoes with green chile peppers
1 (28oz) can whole peeled tomatoes

Preheat oven to 400 degrees F. Place jalapeño chile peppers on a medium baking sheet. Bake for 15 minutes or until roasted. Remove from heat and chop off stems.

Place jalapeño peppers, garlic, onion, white sugar, salt, ground cumin and diced tomatoes with green chilies in blender or food processor. Chop using the pulse setting for a few seconds. Mix in whole peeled tomatoes. Chop using the pulse setting to attain desired consistency. Black pepper to taste and then transfer to a medium bowl and cover. Chill for at least 45 minutes prior to serving. Yields about 2 to 3 cups.

Atomic Salsa

10 lbs ripe red tomatoes
1 1/2 lbs green bell peppers, diced
1 lb red bell peppers, diced
12 jalapeño peppers, seeded
and minced
3 habanero peppers, seeded
and minced
1 lb green chile peppers, diced
1 lb red onions, chopped

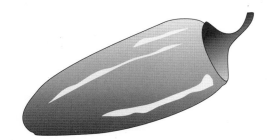

In a large saucepan, fill 2/3 with hot water. Bring to a boil and blanch tomatoes. Drain and rinse with cold water. Peel and chop into 1/2 inch size squares. Place tomatoes in a large saucepan with enough water to just cover. Bring to a boil and reduce heat to a simmer. In another large saucepan, bring approximately 2 quarts of lightly salted water to boil. Place green and red bell peppers, jalapeño peppers, habanero chilies, green chile peppers, onions and garlic in boiling water. Cook until tender, about 15 minutes. Drain vegetables and stir into saucepan with tomatoes. Mix in white sugar, ground black pepper and chopped cilantro. Simmer 15 to 20 minutes, stirring occasionally. Add more water if necessary to obtain desired consistency. Store in refrigerator prior to serving. Yields about 8 cups.

Chiltepine Salsa

1 (16oz) can diced tomatoes with green chilies
3 green onions, coarsely chopped
2 cloves garlic, chopped finely
1 tsp Mexican oregano
1 Tbl chili powder, more to taste
10 dried Chiltepine peppers
2 lemons, juiced
Salt and pepper to taste

Place all ingredients in blender and mix until smooth. Mixture should be well processed. Taste of salsa improves with age. Refrigerate for storage.
Yields about 2 cups.

Chile Pepper Salsa

1 large red onion, diced
1/2 c white onion, diced
10 large tomatoes, peeled and chopped
2 large green bell peppers, diced
1 large red bell pepper, diced
2 Anaheim chile peppers, diced
2 banana peppers, diced
4 jalapeño peppers, diced
1 (28oz) can tomato sauce
1 (6oz) can tomato paste

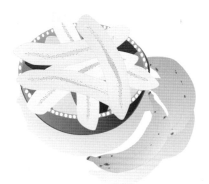

In a large pot mix onions, tomatoes, green bell peppers, red bell pepper, Anaheim chilies, banana peppers and jalapeño peppers. Stir in tomato sauce, tomato paste, vinegar, diced tomatoes and brown sugar. Season with chili powder, Italian seasoning, salt and black pepper. Bring to a boil, reduce heat to low and simmer for 1 hour. Mix the cornstarch and water and then stir into the salsa to thicken. Transfer salsa to sterilized jars, leaving 1/2 inch headroom and seal. Process jars in a boiling water bath for 15 minutes. Store unsealed jars in the refrigerator.
Yields about 8 cups.

Green Chile and Tomato Salsa

12 firm tomatoes, diced
1 medium red onion, diced
1 small can diced green chilies
6 medium cloves garlic, diced finely
3 jalapeño chile peppers, sliced and diced
1 habanero chile pepper, diced finely
1 bunch of cilantro, shredded
3 medium avocados, seeded, peeled and chopped
3 limes, juiced
Salt and pepper to taste

Mix all ingredients in a large bowl and season to taste.
Refrigerate until ready to serve.
Yields about 4 cups.

Blackened Tomato Chipotle Salsa

1/4 c plus 1 Tbl olive oil
1 small red onion, chopped finely
2 lbs plum tomatoes, blackened
1 clove garlic, minced
1/2 c fresh cilantro, chopped
4 chipotle chilies en adobo, chopped
1/4 c red wine vinegar
1 Tbl salt
1 tsp white sugar
2 Tbl lemon pepper

Heat broiler. Cut tomatoes in half and blacken in broiler. Allow to cool and then dice 1/2 the blackened tomatoes. Set both diced and halved tomatoes aside.

Heat a tablespoon of olive oil in a sauté pan over medium heat until lightly smoking. Sauté onion until caramelized, about 10 minutes.

Place caramelized onions and 1/2 the blackened tomatoes in food processor or blender and pulse until finely chopped but not pureed. Add cilantro and chipotle chilies and pulse again to mix.

Peel, seed and chop remaining tomatoes and fold together with remaining 1/4 c olive oil, vinegar, salt, sugar and lemon pepper.

Yields about 4 cups.

Roasted Corn and Onion Salsa

2 ears corn in husks (about 1 1/4 pounds)
1 Tbl vegetable or olive oil
1 c yellow onion, chopped
1/2 c cilantro leaves, chopped coarsely
3 Tbl fresh lime juice
1 tsp sugar
11/2 tsp cumin seeds, bruised in mortar
1 tsp bottled crushed red pepper flakes
   or 1 or 2 Tbl fresh chilies, minced
2 to 3 Tbl dried chipotles, canned in adobo sauce
1 to 2 tsp adobo sauce

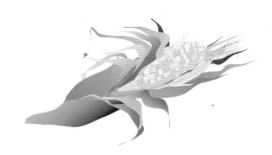

Husk corn and cut kernels from cob using long-bladed knife (yields about 2 cups). Heat oil in large skillet over high heat. Add corn and sauté for about 2 minutes or until it gets some golden patches. Add onions and sauté 1 minute longer. Remove from heat and combine with all other ingredients in bowl. Makes 12 servings or 3 cups.

This recipe is courtesy of the National Onion Association.

Avocado and Corn Salsa

3/4 c olive oil
4 cups fresh corn kernels (about 5 ears)
2 avocados, peeled, pitted and chopped
1 large red bell pepper, cored, seeded and diced
1 large yellow bell pepper, cored, seeded and diced
 4 Poblano chilies, roasted, peeled, seeded and diced
4 scallions, thinly sliced on the diagonal
1/2 c red wine vinegar
Salt and pepper to taste

Heat olive oil in a large skillet over medium heat. Sauté corn about 5 minutes, or until lightly browned. Lightly season with salt and pepper. Transfer seasoned corn to a large mixing bowl. Add avocados, bell peppers, scallions and red wine vinegar to corn. Salt and pepper to taste and let sit 20 to 30 minutes to blend the flavors.

Black Bean Pepper Salsa

3/4 c dried black beans, washed
1 tsp salt
1 red bell pepper, roasted, seeded, peeled and diced
1 yellow bell pepper, roasted, seeded, peeled and diced
2 chipotle chilies in adobo, minced
2 tsp orange zest, minced
2 Tbl fresh cilantro, chopped
2 Tbl sherry vinegar
2 Tbl extra virgin olive oil

Cook beans for 1 to 1 1/2 hours or until tender, adding a teaspoon of salt towards the end. Drain the beans, allow to cool and then transfer to a mixing bowl.
Add remaining 1/2 tsp salt and the rest of the ingredients and mix well. Yields about 2 1/2 cups.

Jalapeño and Sweet Pepper Salsa

1 large garlic clove, minced
1/4 c Tbl olive oil
4 large yellow onions, chopped finely
2 red bell peppers, de-veined, seeded and chopped
5 jalapeño peppers, seeded and chopped finely
6 medium tomatoes, diced
1 (28oz) can tomato sauce
1 (13oz) can tomato paste
2 lemons, juiced
1 bunch fresh cilantro, chopped
Chili powder to taste
Oregano to taste
Salt and pepper to taste

Heat olive oil in a large pot over medium/low heat. Add garlic and sauté for about 2 minutes, until just softened. Add onions and sauté until translucent. Add chili powder, oregano and cilantro. Continue cooking, stirring constantly until mixture is soft. Add tomatoes, tomato sauce, tomato paste and lemon juice to the pot. Let simmer for about 8 minutes. Cool and serve.

Charred Habanero Salsa

6 plum tomatoes, halved
5 Tbl olive oil
4 cloves garlic, crushed
10 habanero chilies, roasted
1 large red onion, chopped finely
3 Tbl fresh cilantro
3 limes, juiced
Salt and pepper to taste

Preheat oven to 475 degrees F. Place tomatoes, cut side up on a baking sheet and drizzle with 1 tablespoon of olive oil. Sprinkle with some garlic, salt and pepper. Roast for about 15 minutes until they begin to char. Meanwhile, charcoal-grill the habaneros until they are blistered, turning once. Dice the tomatoes and habanero chilies and mix with all other ingredients. Salt and pepper to taste.

Spice Up Your Life With a Salsa Garden

Grow your own ingredients for the freshest, most accessible salsa around. The main ingredients to most salsa recipes grow well together, enjoy regular sunlight and well irrigated soils. Here are some tips to make your garden grow.

The tomato likes space. They grow rapidly so give them room to grow in every direction. A sturdy wire cage adds space, giving the tomatoes the ability to grow up as well as out. Prepare your soil by tilling it, then apply fertilizer and work it into the soil. When transplanting tomatoes, make sure you cover the root ball. Seed packets or the little stakes that come with tomato plants contain directions that will explain how far apart each variety should be planted. As for watering, keep the soil moist around the root areas. A general rule of thumb is 1/2 inch of water twice a week during dry periods.

Peppers really like sunlight so they need to be planted where they can get at least 6 hours of sunlight every day. When they are first transplanted peppers need a lot of water but once they are established they are remarkably drought-resistant. They also prefer well-drained soil so raised beds work very well.

Yellow, white and red/purple onions grow very well in full sunlight and well-drained soils as well. To prepare the soil work it 8 to 10 inches deep by breaking up clods, removing rocks and raking the soil smooth. The soil should be fertilized over the top 3 to 4 inches. Onions are a cool season crop so they can stand freezing temperatures. When seeding onions for bulbs, plant them about 1/4 inch deep during October through December. Place seeds 1 inch apart. When the plants are about 1 1/2inches high, thin them to every 2 to 3 inches. You can eat the extra plants as green onions. Watering once a week is usually enough but more may be needed during dry, windy weather. Water slowly and deeply to encourage strong, healthy roots. Onions seeded in October/December or transplants planted in January/February should produce bulbs in May/July. Onions are ready when the main stem begins to weaken and fall.

Don't forget that variety is the spice of life so plant several different kinds of tomatoes, peppers and onions!

Medium

Bell Pepper Salsa

5 large red tomatoes, diced
1 large red onion, diced
1/2 white onion, diced
1 garlic clove, minced
1 green bell pepper, seeded and diced
1/2 red, yellow and orange bell peppers,
   seeded and diced
4 jalapeños, diced
1 bunch cilantro, chopped
1 lime, juiced
1/2 tsp black pepper
1/2 tsp celery salt
1 (8oz) can tomato sauce
Salt and freshly ground black pepper to taste

In a bowl combine all ingredients. Season with salt and freshly ground black pepper to taste. Refrigerate until ready to serve.
Yields about 4 cups.

Tomato-Pineapple Salsa

1 (14.5oz) can diced tomatoes
1/2 c fresh pineapple, diced finely
1/3 c green onions, sliced finely
1/2 tsp jalapeño peppers, seeded and
chopped finely
1 1/2 Tbl fresh cilantro, chopped
1 1/2 Tbl fresh lemon juice
1 clove garlic, chopped finely

Measure all ingredients into large mixing
bowl and stir gently until well mixed.
Serve with grilled or broiled fish or
chicken.

This recipe is courtesy of the California Tomato Growers Association.

Baby Carrot Salsa

1/2 c baby carrots, diced
1 Tbl red onion, diced finely
1 Tbl red bell pepper, diced finely
1 Tbl yellow bell pepper, diced finely
2 Tbl fresh cilantro, chopped
1 green chile peppers, diced finely
1 Tbl fresh lemon juice
1/8 tsp salt
1/2 tsp freshly ground black pepper

In a glass mixing bowl combine carrots, red onion, red and yellow bell peppers, cilantro, green chili, fresh lemon juice, salt and pepper. Cover with plastic wrap and refrigerate for 30 minutes prior to serving.
Yields about 2 cups.

Tomatillo Green Chile Salsa

1 (11oz) can tomatillos, drained
1/2 c white onion, diced
1/2 c red onion, diced
2 cloves garlic, minced
3 green chilies, minced with seeds
1/4 c fresh cilantro, chopped
2 Tbl sugar
1/2 tsp salt
1/2 tsp freshly ground black pepper

In a saucepan on medium/low heat, combine tomatillos, onions, garlic and chilies.
Simmer for 3 minutes or until the tomatillos are soft. Add the sugar and salt, mixing well.
In a glass bowl, cover and refrigerate for 30 minutes prior to serving.
Yields about 2 cups.

Cucumber Tomato Salsa

2 medium cucumbers, peeled, seeded and chopped
2 medium red tomatoes, chopped
1/2 c green bell pepper, chopped
1 jalapeño pepper, minced
1 small white onion, chopped
1 clove garlic, minced
2 Tbl fresh lime juice
1 tsp fresh parsley, minced
1/2 tsp dried dill weed
1/2 tsp salt

In a medium bowl stir together cucumbers, tomatoes, green bell pepper, jalapeño pepper, onion, garlic, lime juice, parsley, cilantro, dill and salt. Cover and refrigerate for 1 hour. Serve with tortilla chips.
Yields about 2 to 3 cups.

Jalapeño Garlic Salsa

2 medium red tomatoes, chopped finely
1 medium red onion, chopped finely
2 jalapeño peppers, chopped finely
2 cloves garlic, minced
1/4 c fresh cilantro, chopped
3 Tbl olive oil
3 Tbl red wine vinegar
1 Tbl lemon juice
Salt and freshly ground black pepper to taste

In a large glass bowl, mix tomatoes, red onion, jalapeños, garlic, cilantro, olive oil, vinegar, lemon juice, salt and black pepper. Let stand for 30 minutes prior to serving. Yields about 2 cups.

Multi Pepper Salsa

3 long green Anaheim peppers, de-veined, chopped with seeds
2 yellow bell peppers, de-veined, seeded and minced
2 jalapeño peppers, chopped
1 serrano pepper, chopped
6 large tomatoes, chopped
3 green onions, chopped
1 clove garlic, minced
1/4 c olive oil
2 limes, juiced

Mix all ingredients in a bowl and chill for 1 hour before serving. Yields about 3 to 4 cups.

Tabasco and Red Wine Salsa

3 lbs Roma tomatoes, seeded and chopped coarsely
1/4 lb jalapeño peppers, seeded and chopped finely
3/4 lb Maui onions, chopped finely
3 bunches fresh cilantro, chopped finely
2 tsp dry granulated garlic
1 tsp Tabasco Sauce
2 Tbl olive oil
3 Tbl red wine vinegar
4 limes, juiced
1/2 tsp black pepper
1 Tbl garlic salt
3 avocados, peeled, pitted and diced

Mix all of the above ingredients, except the avocados. When ready to serve, add avocados, salt and Tabasco to taste.
Yields about 4 to 5 cups.

Sweet Carrot Salsa

2 carrots, chopped
1 red onion, diced
1 tsp garlic, minced
4 unseeded jalapeños, chopped
1 red bell pepper, de-veined, seeded and chopped
1 bunch fresh cilantro, chopped
3 Tbl lemon juice
3 large red tomatoes, diced
1/4 c fresh orange juice

Place tomatoes in food processor and mix until fine. Add onion, garlic, jalapeños, bell pepper, cilantro, lemon juice and orange juice. Process until mixed well. Add tomatoes and process only for a few seconds so salsa remains chunky. Serve.
Yields about 2 to 3 cups.

Black and White Salsa

1 c black beans, cooked and drained
1 c Great Northern beans, cooked and drained
1 c red tomatoes, diced
3 Tbl white wine vinegar
1/4 c fresh cilantro, chopped
1/4 c red onion, chopped
1/4 c white onion, chopped
2 Tbl jalapeño pepper, chopped
2 cloves garlic, minced
1/2 tsp sugar
Salt and pepper to taste

In a medium bowl combine all ingredients. Season to taste and let sit for 30 minutes. Serve. Yields about 3 cups.

Black-eyed Pea Salsa

2 medium red tomatoes, seeded and chopped

1 (15oz) can black-eyed peas, rinsed and drained
1 medium green pepper, de-veined and chopped
1/2 c green onion, sliced
1/2 c fresh cilantro, chopped
2 Tbl lemon juice
1 jalapeño pepper, seeded and finely chopped
2 cloves garlic, minced
1/4 tsp ground cumin
1/2 tsp salt
1 tsp garlic powder
Black pepper to taste

Combine all ingredients in bowl and mix well. Cover and chill at least 4 hours prior to serving. Yields about 3 cups.

Cabbage Salsa

2 c shredded savoy cabbage
8 red radishes, diced
6 scallions, white and pale green parts only, sliced thinly
1 serrano chile, minced
1/4 c fresh lime juice
2 Tbl rice vinegar
2 Tbl olive oil
1/4 cup fresh cilantro, chopped
Salt and freshly ground black pepper to taste

In a medium bowl toss together the cabbage, carrots, radishes, scallions and Serrano chile. Pour the lime juice, vinegar and olive oil over the vegetables and toss gently but thoroughly. Salt and pepper to taste and add chopped cilantro. Mix thoroughly again and let sit at room temperature for 1 hour prior to serving.
Yields about 3 to 4 cups.

Charred Red Onion Salsa

3 medium red onions, skin on, halved
1/4 c olive oil
1/4 c balsamic vinegar
2 Tbl white wine vinegar
1 tsp bottled crushed red pepper flakes
1 c whole pitted olives
2 Tbl fresh oregano leaves (packed)

Place onion halves cut sides down in shallow pan. Bake at 425 degrees for 30 minutes or until onions are slightly soft when pinched and their cut sides are blackened. When cool enough to handle discard onion skins and trim stems. Place onions in food processor with oil, vinegars and red pepper flakes. Process in two or three 2-second bursts or until coarsely chopped. Add olives and oregano and process 2 to 4 seconds just until chopped. Makes 12 servings or 3 cups.

This recipe is courtesy of the National Onion Association.

Teaching Health

Healthy eating is a learned habit. Learning how to eat the right foods the first time around can save a child from the fad-diet merry-go-round lifestyle that so many adults live today. Good nutrition and a healthy diet help a child to grow up healthy. Better bones, eyes, skin and teeth can all be easily accomplished by teaching smart eating habits. Some tried and true family strategies are:

* Eat meals together as a family
* Serve a colorful variety of healthy foods and snacks
* Be a role model; healthy parents make healthy kids
* Involve children in the process
* Make healthy foods easily accessible

Developing the routine of eating meals together as a family can be difficult with busy schedules of work,school, sports, tutoring and friends. Routine is the key word. Make it a daily occurrence and the juggling of time, duties and schedules will work themselves out.

The 5-a-day for Better Health program is a public/private nutrition education initiative that is working to increase fruit and vegetable consumption to 5 a day for 75 percent of Americans by 2010. They suggest that eating a colorful variety of fruits and vegetables needs to be part of an everyday diet because the deeply hued fruits and vegetables provide the necessary range of vitamins, minerals, fiber and phytochemicals a body needs to maintain good health and energy levels. See their Web site at www.5aday.org for more detailed information.

Modeling a healthy eating lifestyle will result in children following suit with better eating habits. Developing a taste from infancy for fresh fruits and raw vegetables and learning how to cook and prepare healthy snacks and meals is a life-long gift that a caring parent can give their child. Not having to battle unnecessary weight-problems, teeth, bone or skin problems, even as simple as acne from too much fried food, is a gift and a blessing. Children are visual and tactile learners. Watching an adult's eating habits is the number one way they learn how to eat.

Tactile learning is the other main way kids learn and they like to get their hands dirty. There are so many cooking projects kids can do and it can be a fun family project. The basic skills of preparing food and planning healthy meals will last a lifetime.

Having a variety of healthy foods easily accessible makes eating healthier foods an easy option. Many families today are so busy, fast food and prepackaged snacks fill cupboards to bursting. Fresh fruits and vegetables kept washed and ready to eat make great "fast food" snacks. Dips like salsa and guacamole give an extra kick to turn these snacks into treats that kids and adults will crave.

Take the time to make the habit of healthy living. Be a role model and give the gift of health. For more tips and recipes, go to the Viva Tortilla Web site at www.vivatortilla.com.

Fruity-Tooty Salsa

2 c fresh pineapple chunks, chopped
1 kiwi, peeled and chopped coarsely
1 large orange, peeled and chopped coarsely
3/4 c raisins
1/4 c fresh cilantro, chopped finely
1 Tbl fresh lime juice
1 Tbl honey

In a medium bowl combine all ingredients and stir well. Refrigerate at least one hour before serving. Serve with cinnamon crisps or browned and buttered warm tortillas.

Mild

Adobo Salsa

1 (28oz) can diced tomatoes
1 green bell pepper, diced
1/4 c red onion, diced
1/4 c fresh cilantro, chopped
1 Tbl adobo sauce from canned chipotle peppers
1 Tbl fresh tarragon, chopped
1/2 tsp salt
2 Tbl balsamic vinegar
Black pepper to taste

In a bowl, toss together the tomatoes, bell pepper, onion, cilantro adobo sauce, tarragon and vinegar. Add salt and season to taste with black pepper. Cover and refrigerate for at least 30 minutes prior to serving.
Yields about 2 cups.

Black Bean and Corn Salsa

1 (15oz) can black beans, rinsed and drained
1 c corn kernels
1/2 c red bell pepper, chopped
1/2 c fresh cilantro, chopped
3 Tbl lime juice
8 small green onions, chopped
2 Tbl balsamic vinegar
1/2 tsp ground cumin
1 small green chile, chopped finely

Combine all ingredients in bowl and refrigerate overnight.
Yields about 2 to 3 cups.

Green Chile Cilantro Salsa

6 medium red tomatoes
2 cloves garlic, diced
1 red onion, chopped finely
1/3 c roasted New Mexico green chilies, chopped
3 Tbl fresh cilantro, chopped
1 Tbl fresh lime juice
1/4 tsp salt

Cut tomatoes in half and then on a grill or under broiler, roast or brown the tomatoes. Place roasted tomatoes in bowl to cool. Once they are cool enough to touch, chop them coarsely and place in a large bowl. Add garlic, onion, chilies, cilantro, lime juice and salt.

Mix all ingredients, cover and place in refrigerate. Allow to chill at least 30 minutes prior to serving.

Yields about 3 cups.

Plum Tomato Salsa

8 plum tomatoes, seeded and chopped
6 green onions, sliced
1/4 c fresh cilantro, chopped
1/2 tsp ground black pepper
2 Tbl olive oil
1/4 c balsamic vinegar
1 tsp salt

In a medium bowl, combine tomatoes, green onions, cilantro, pepper, olive oil, balsamic vinegar and salt. Wrap the bowl with plastic wrap and refrigerate for 1 hour prior to serving.
Yields about 2 to 3 cups.

Green Olive Salsa

2 large tomatoes, finely chopped
5 green onions, chopped
3 Tbl olive oil
3 1/2 Tbl tarragon vinegar
1 (4oz) can chopped green chili peppers
1/3 c green olives, chopped
1 tsp garlic salt
1 tsp salt
Pepper to taste

In a medium bowl mix together tomatoes, green onions, olive oil, tarragon vinegar, green chili peppers, green olives, garlic salt, salt and black pepper. Cover and refrigerate for several hours prior to serving.
Yields about 2 cups.

Salsa Verde

1 c onion, chopped finely
1/4 c olive oil
1 1/2 c spinach, chopped
1 1/2 c whole tomatillos, cooked
1/2 c green chilies, chopped
2 cloves garlic, crushed
1 Tbl dried oregano leaves
1 c vegetable broth

Cook and stir onions in oil in 3 quart saucepan until tender. Add spinach, tomatillos with liquid, garlic and oregano. Cover and cook over medium heat 5 minutes. Transfer to blender, cover and blend on low speed until smooth, about 1 minute. Return mixture to saucepan; stir in vegetable broth. Heat to boiling; reduce heat and simmer, uncovered, for 10 minutes. Cover and refrigerate until ready to serve.
Yields about 4 1/2 cups.

Canned Tomatillo Salsa

1 (11oz) can tomatillo, drained
1/2 c white onion, diced
2 cloves garlic, minced
3 green chilies, minced with seeds
1/4 c fresh cilantro, chopped
2 Tbl sugar
1/2 tsp salt
1/2 tsp freshly ground black pepper

In a medium bowl combine tomatillo, garlic, chilies, cilantro, sugar, salt and pepper. Cover with plastic wrap and place in refrigerator for 1 hour to blend flavors.
Yields about 1 1/2 cups.

Artichoke Heart Salsa

1 (6.5oz) jar marinated artichoke hearts,
drained and chopped
3 plum tomatoes, chopped
2 Tbl red onion, chopped
1/4 c black olives, chopped
1 Tbl garlic, chopped
2 Tbl fresh basil, chopped
Salt and pepper to taste

In a medium bowl mix together artichoke hearts, tomatoes, onion, olives, garlic, salt and pepper. Serve chilled or at room temperature.
Yields about 2 cups.

Cottage Cheese Salsa

1 ear corn, husked and cleaned
1 (15oz) can black beans
1 (32oz) container low-fat cottage cheese
1 ripe avocado, peeled, pitted and diced
2 plum tomatoes, seeded and diced
2 Tbl fresh lime juice
1/4 c red onion, chopped
3 Tbl olive oil
3 Tbl fresh cilantro, chopped
2 jalapeños, minced
Salt and freshly ground black pepper to taste.

Boil corn on the cob in a medium saucepan over medium/high heat until tender, about 15 minutes. Cool under running water and slice kernels from cob. Set aside.

Cook the black beans in a small saucepan over medium heat until warm and tender, about 10 minutes. Strain and rinse under cold water. Set aside.

Place cottage cheese in a serving bowl. Add avocados, tomatoes, black beans, corn, lime juice, red onion, olive oil, cilantro and jalapeños. Season to taste with salt and black pepper. Mix well, cover and refrigerate until ready to serve. Yields about 3 to 4 cups.

Chunky Black Bean and Corn Salsa

1/3 c olive oil
2 small jalapeño peppers, seeded and finely minced
1 small red onion, chopped finely
1 large red tomato, chopped
1/2 c fresh cilantro, chopped finely
1/4 c fresh lime juice
1 clove garlic, minced
1/2 tsp ground cumin
1/2 tsp ground coriander
2 c black beans, cooked and drained
2 c corn kernels
1 small red bell pepper, seeded and chopped
1 small orange bell pepper, seeded and chopped
Salt and freshly ground black pepper to taste.

Mix all ingredients together in a bowl and season to taste with salt and freshly ground black pepper. Refrigerate for two hours prior to serving.
Yields about 4 to 5 cups.

Eggplant Salsa

4 medium eggplants
1 large red bell pepper, halved and seeded
4 large tomatoes, seeded and diced
1 clove garlic, chopped
1 lime, juiced
Salt and pepper to taste
1/4 c fresh cilantro, chopped
1/4 c olive oil

Preheat oven to 400 degrees F. Slice the tops off the eggplants, and place on a baking sheet with red pepper halves. Drizzle with olive oil to lightly coat.

Bake for about 40 minutes or until eggplant is tender. Remove from the oven and place eggplant and peppers into a large resealable bag. Seal and let sit for 15 minutes to loosen the skin. Remove from bag, peel off skins and dice eggplants and pepper. Transfer to a large bowl.

Place tomatoes and garlic in bowl with roasted vegetables and season with salt, pepper and cilantro. Mix well and set aside.

Goes very well with toasted pita bread.

Yields about 3 cups.

Tips on blackening tomatoes and tomatillos:

Remove stems. Tomatillos need to be husked and rinsed.
- Place on broiler rack or over gas flame.
- Heat until skins blister, crack and blacken.
- After blackening tomatoes and tomatillos they can be placed in a plastic or paper bag and left to steam for about 15 minutes. Skins will remove easily after loosened.
- Blackening gives tomatoes and tomatillos a more rustic, complex flavor.
- Do not over-blacken or taste will become bitter.

Tips on oven roasting tomatoes:

Preheat oven to 250 degrees F.
- Cut tomatoes in half and place cut side up on a wire rack or baking sheet.
- Sprinkle with a little salt or lightly brush with olive oil.
- Roast in the oven for about 3 hours.
- Roast fresh garlic in middle of sliced tomatoes for extra flavor. Discard garlic after roasting.
- If not using immediately, store roasted tomatoes in a sealed jar in olive oil.
- Roasting removes excess moisture from tomatoes and concentrates the flavor.

Tips on roasting chilies and bell peppers

Place chilies or bell peppers on a wire rack over an open gas flame or grill, or under a broiler.
- Blister and blacken the skins all over without burning the flesh.
- Skins can be bitter so they are often removed.
- Let roasted chilies or bell peppers steam in a sealed plastic bag or bowl for about 15 minutes to loosen skin.
- Skin should remove easily after steaming. Use fingers or the tip of a knife.
- Roasting chilies or bell peppers concentrates their flavors, adding a more robust, smoky flavor.

Tips on toasting and rehydrating dried chilies:

Stem and seed dried chilies.
- Dry-roast them in a single layer in dry cast-iron skillet or on a baking sheet in a 250-degree oven for 2 to 3 minutes.
- Shake occasionally and do not allow them to burn or blacken.
- Transfer chilies to a bowl and add enough hot water to just cover.
- Let stand for about 20 minutes until they are rehydrated and soft.

Fruit
Salsas

Hot

Apple Habanero Salsa

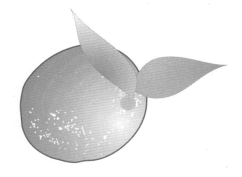

2 Apples, diced into small pieces
2 habanero chilies, seeded and diced
1/2 red onion, diced
1/4 c fresh cilantro, chopped
2 limes, juiced
 Salt and pepper to taste

Place habanero chilies, red onion, cilantro and lime in food processor and mix well. Add apple pieces and process to chunky texture. Salt and pepper to taste. Yields about 2 cups.

Caramelized Pineapple Salsa

1 ripe pineapple, peeled, cored and cut into 1/4-inch thick slices
1/2 c red bell pepper, seeded and diced
2 tsp chipotle chile pepper, pureed
2 Tbl fresh orange juice
3 Tbl fresh lime juice
1 Tbl fresh cilantro, chopped
2 tsp light brown sugar
1/4 tsp chili powder

Saute pineapple slices in a large skillet over medium/high heat until both sides are lightly browned, about 5 to 8 minutes per side. Dice the browned pineapple and transfer to a mixing bowl.
Place chipotle pepper into a food processor and puree until it forms a paste.
Add remaining ingredients to diced pineapples and combine thoroughly.

Yields about 3 cups.

Serrano Pineapple Salsa

2 c fresh pineapple, diced
2 Tbl red bell pepper, seeded
    and chopped finely
2 tsp Serrano chilies, minced with seeds
3 Tbl fresh cilantro, chopped
1 tsp white sugar
2 Tbl balsamic vinegar
1/4 tsp chili powder

Combine all ingredients in a large mixing bowl and mix thoroughly. Refrigerate until ready to serve.

Yields about 2 to 3 cups.

Eggplant Scallion Salsa

2 red bell peppers, seeded and chopped finely
2 stalks celery, chopped finely
2 red Fresno chilies, chopped finely with seeds
1/2 white onion, chopped finely
1 large clove garlic, minced
1 bay leaf
1 sprig fresh thyme
Hot pepper sauce to taste
3/4 c water
3/4 c olive oil
8 oz eggplant, peeled and diced
3 scallions, green ends removed, sliced lengthwise
1 tsp fresh basil
1 Tbl olive oil

Place the bell pepper, celery, chilies, onion, garlic, herbs, salt, hot pepper sauce and water in a medium saucepan and cook uncovered over medium/high heat for about 10 minutes or until water evaporates. Remove from heat, discard bay leaf and thyme, transfer to a mixing bowl and leave to cool.

Heat the 1/2 cup olive oil in a large skillet and sauté the eggplant over medium heat until tender, about 5 to 6 minutes. Transfer to mixing bowl. Add tomatoes, scallions, thyme and olive oil. Combine all ingredients and mix thoroughly.

Yields about 2 cups.

Habanero Mango Salsa

1 ripe avocado, peeled, pitted and diced

1 lime, juiced
1 mango, peeled, seeded and diced
1 small red onion, chopped
1 habanero pepper, seeded and chopped
1 Tbl fresh cilantro, chopped
1/2 tsp chili powder
Salt and freshly ground black pepper to taste

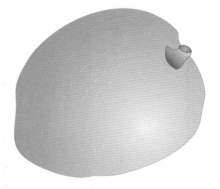

Mix diced avocado and lime juice in a medium
bowl. Add mango, onion, habanero pepper,
cilantro, chili powder and mix thoroughly. Salt
and pepper to taste.
Serve at room temperature.
Yields about 2 cups.

Habanero Papaya Salsa

1 fresh yellow habanero chili,
   seeded and stemmed
1 yellow tomato, chopped coarsely
3 papayas, peeled and chopped coarsely
3/4 c fresh orange juice
2 Tbl fresh lime juice
1 Tbl rice wine vinegar
1 Tbl water
1 tsp sugar
Salt and freshly ground pepper to taste

Place all ingredients in a food processor or blender and puree. Refrigerate until ready to serve.
Yields about 2 to 3 cups.

Hot Pepper Mango Salsa

1 c red onion, sliced finely
2 cloves garlic, minced
3 plum tomatoes, diced
4 Serrano chilies, minced with seeds
1 c fresh pineapple, diced
1 (14oz) can coconut milk
1 tsp Achiote paste
1 bunch fresh cilantro, tied
1 mango, peeled, pitted and sliced
2 Tbl fresh cilantro, chopped
2 Tbl fresh lime juice
Hot pepper sauce to taste

In a saucepan, cook onion, garlic, tomatoes, chilies, pineapple, coconut mild, achiote and cilantro over medium/high heat, uncovered for about 10 minutes. Remove tied cilantro and cook another 8 to 10 minutes until mixture thickens. Transfer to a blender and puree to desired consistency. Place blender jar in refrigerator.

When chilled, discard 1 cup of liquid. Add mango, chopped cilantro, lime juice and hot sauce to blender and mix until desired consistency is reached. Transfer to serving bowl. Goes very well with fish or seafood.

Yields about 2 cups.

Adobo Peach Salsa

1 c sliced canned peaches, drained and chopped
1/3 c red onion, chopped
2 cloves garlic, minced
1 1/2 tsp fresh ginger root, minced
2 tsp minced chipotle peppers in adobo sauce
1/3 c fresh cilantro, chopped
1/2 lime, juiced
Salt and freshly ground black pepper to taste

In a medium bowl, mix peaches, onion, garlic, ginger, chipotle peppers in adobo sauce, cilantro and lime. Season with salt and ground black pepper. Chill until serving. Yields about 1 1/2 cups.

Peach Pepperoncini Salsa

2 ears fresh corn, husked
1 large red tomato, chopped
1 large peach, pitted and chopped
1 red onion, chopped
6 pepperoncini peppers, chopped
1 Tbl green chili pepper, chopped
Garlic salt and black pepper to taste

Bring a large pot of water to boil. Boil corn for 5 minutes, or until kernels are tender. Drain corn, cool and cut kernels from cob. In a food processor pulse the tomato, peach, red onion, pepperoncini peppers, green chili pepper, garlic salt and pepper until chunky. Transfer to a bowl and mix in the corn. Chill in refrigerator until ready to serve. Yields about 1 to 2 cups.

Jalapeño Cactus Salsa

1 (16oz) jar nopales, drained, rinsed and dried
2 c red tomatoes, chopped
1/2 white onion, diced
5 jalapeño peppers, minced
1/2 c fresh cilantro, chopped coarsely
2 lemons, juiced
1/2 tsp garlic salt
Ground black pepper to taste

In a medium mixing bowl, combine cactus, tomatoes, onions, jalapeños, cilantro and garlic salt.
Black pepper to taste. Juice both lemons over the
mixture. Cover and refrigerate for at least one
hour prior to serving.
Yields about 1 to 2 cups.

Peach Onion Salsa

1/2 c yellow onion, chopped
2 c ripe peaches, pitted and chopped
3 Tbl fresh cilantro, chopped
2 Tbl jalapeño pepper, chopped
Salt
Fresh lime juice

Combine all ingredients in a medium bowl, adding salt and lime juice to taste; cover and refrigerate until ready to serve.

Makes 6 servings.

This recipe is courtesy of the National Onion Association.

Habanero Fruit Salsa

5 kiwis, peeled and diced
1 quart strawberries, chopped finely
1 pint fresh blackberries, chopped
4 green apples, peeled, cored
   and coarsely shredded
2 Tbl preserves, flavor of choice
3/4 c brown sugar
1 Tbl cayenne pepper
3 Tbl habanero hot sauce
1 (7oz) can green salsa
1/3 c fresh lime juice
Freshly ground black pepper to taste

Place kiwis, strawberries, blackberries and apples in a bowl. Stir in jelly, brown sugar, cayenne pepper, hot sauce, green salsa and lime juice. Season to taste with black pepper. Mix thoroughly. Refrigerate until serving.

Yields about 3 to 4 cups.

Serrano Fruit Salsa

2 c mango, diced
2 c fresh peaches, pitted and chopped
2 cloves garlic, minced
2 Tbl fresh ginger root, chopped
1/4 c fresh basil, chopped
2 Serrano chile peppers, diced
1/4 c fresh lime juice
1 tsp honey

In a large bowl mix together mangoes, peaches, garlic, ginger and basil. Add the chilies, lime juice and honey and mix thoroughly. Allow to chill 2 hours before serving.

Yields about 2 to 3 cups.

Anaheim Watermelon Salsa

2 c watermelon, seeded and chopped coarsely
2 Tbl red onion, chopped
3 Tbl Anaheim chile, seeded and chopped
2 Tbl balsamic vinegar
Salt and freshly ground black pepper to taste

In a serving bowl, mix together watermelon, onion and chile pepper. Season with balsamic vinegar, salt and black pepper. Cover and refrigerate for at least 1 hour to blend flavors.

Yields about 2 to 3 cups.

Medium

Black Bean Mango Salsa

2 cans (15 3/4 oz ea.) black beans, drained and rinsed
2 oranges, peeled, seeded and chopped
2 mangoes, peeled, pitted and chopped
1 red bell pepper, de-veined, seeded and chopped
3 Serrano chilies, seeded and thinly sliced
2 Tbl fresh lime juice
2 Tbl fresh cilantro, chopped
1 tsp fresh ginger, grated
Salt and freshly ground black pepper to taste

Combine beans, orange, mango, red bell pepper, Serrano
chilies, lime juice, cilantro, salt and pepper in a large bowl.
For best flavor, refrigerate, covered for at least 2 hours.

Yields about 2 to 3 cups.

Peach Salsa

2 (15oz) cans peaches, drained and chopped
2 green onions, sliced thinly, including tops
2 Tbl fresh lime juice
2 tsp fresh cilantro, chopped
2 tsp Asian garlic chili sauce
1/2 tsp Asian five spice powder
1/4 tsp white pepper

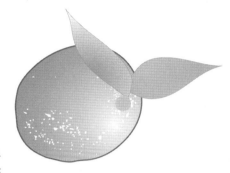

In a medium bowl, combine peaches, green onions, cilantro, garlic chili sauce, lime juice, five spice powder and white pepper. Mix well. Chill before serving.

Yields about 2 cups.

Red Apple Salsa

2 medium red apples, cored and diced
2 Tbl fresh lime juice
1/2 c orange segments, chopped
1/2 c white onion, chopped finely
1/2 c green pepper, chopped finely
1 jalapeño pepper, chopped finely
2 Tbl fresh cilantro, chopped
1 Tbl cider vinegar
1/2 tsp ground cumin
1 tsp olive oil

Immediately after dicing red apples, combine with lime juice. Stir in remaining ingredients. Refrigerate for 2 hours prior to serving.

Yields about 2 to 3 cups.

Black Bean and Papaya Salsa

1 c black beans, cooked and drained
2 ripe papayas, peeled, seeded and diced into small squares
1/2 red bell pepper, de-veined and diced into small squares
1/2 green bell pepper, de-veined and diced into small squares
1/2 red onion, diced into small squares
3/4 c pineapple juice
1/2 c fresh lime juice
1/2 cup fresh cilantro, chopped
2 Tbl ground cumin
1 Tbl Serrano chile, minced
Salt
Fresh cracked black pepper

In a large mixing bowl combine all ingredients and mix together well. Serve chilled or at room temperature.
Yields about 2 cups.

Zesty Apple Salsa

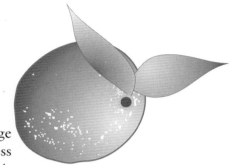

3 large Fuji apples, peeled, halved and cored
1/2 c green onions, minced
2 Tbl jalapeño peppers, seeded and minced
1/2 c fresh lemon juice
2 Tbl honey
4 tsp finely grated lemon peel

Coarsely grate apples into strainer set over large bowl. Press and turn apples to drain off excess juices. Transfer apples to medium bowl and stir in green onions and chilies. Whisk lemon juice, honey and lemon peel in a small bowl and then mix into apples. Salt and pepper to taste. Cover and chill for at least 30 minutes.

Yields about 2 to 3 cups.

Apple and Pear Salsa

2 Tbl fresh lime juice
1/4 c pineapple juice
3 Anjou pears, peeled and diced
3 red apples, peeled and diced
2 Tbl fresh mint, diced
3 Serrano chilies, seeded and minced

Mix the pineapple juice and lime juice in a large bowl. Add the diced pears and apple then toss to cover fruit in juices. Add mint and chilies and mix well. Serve chilled or at room temperature.

Yields about 2 to 3 cups.

Apricot Salsa

1/2 red bell pepper, roasted and chopped
Olive oil
1 small red onion, chopped
1 medium tomato, chopped
1 jalapeño, minced finely
2 apricots, seeded and chopped
2 Tbl dark rum
Dark apple cider

Cut a red bell pepper in half; remove seeds and brush with olive oil. Place the half under broiler very close to the heat until it blackens (about 5 minutes). Remove from heat and chop it.

Sauté the chopped onion in small amount of olive oil until translucent. Add tomato and jalapeño and sauté about another 5 minutes until tomato is cooked. Add apricots and enough cider to cover. Boil down until cider is almost all boiled off. Add roasted bell pepper and stir. Add dark rum and flambé (light and swirl until it goes out).

Yields about 1 to 2 cups.

Avocado Salsa

1 avocado, peeled, pitted and diced
4 small red tomatoes, diced
1 small red onion, diced
1 green pepper, seeded and diced
1 jalapeño, finely diced
1 green chili, finely diced
1 garlic clove, minced
Salt to taste
2 Tbl red wine vinegar
1 Tbl olive oil
4 drops Tabasco sauce

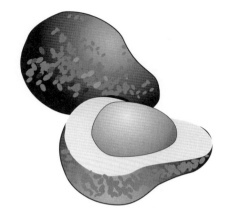

Combine avocado, tomatoes, onion, jalapeño and green chili and mix well. Mash garlic and salt in a small bowl. Add vinegar, oil and Tabasco sauce. Pour this mixture over avocado, tomatoes, onion, jalapeño and green chile and toss. Serve chilled or at room temperature.

Yields about 2 to 3 cups.

Blueberry Salsa

2 Tbl red onion, chopped finely
1 Tbl jalapeño peppers, chopped finely
1 large pink grapefruit, sectioned and diced
1 tsp honey
1 Tbl fresh lime juice
1 c fresh blueberries

Section pink grapefruit and discard membrane. Dice grapefruit and mix with chopped onion, jalapeño pepper, honey and lime juice. Stir in blueberries.

Yields about 1 to 2 cups.

Blueberry Melon Salsa

2 c fresh blueberries
1 c honeydew melon, diced
3 Tbl fresh lime juice
1 c red onion, diced
1/4 c fresh cilantro, chopped
1 Tbl peanut oil
1 tsp grated lime peel
1 jalapeño, minced
Coarse salt to taste

Combine all ingredients and salt to taste.
Let stand one hour then refrigerate until
serving time.
Yields about 2 to 3 cups.

Caribbean Fruit Salsa

1/2 honeydew melon, peeled, seeded and diced
1/2 cantaloupe, peeled, seeded and diced
1/2 pineapple, peeled, cored and diced
1 papaya, peeled and diced
1 mango, peeled and diced
1 red pepper, seeded and diced
1 red onion, diced
1/2 Tbl garlic, chopped
1/2 Tbl ground cumin
1/2 Tbl salt
3 Tbl lime juice
2 Tbl olive oil
1/2 Tbl coarse black pepper
1/2 bunch fresh cilantro, chopped
2 jalapeños, seeded and diced finely

In a large bowl mix all ingredients together. Refrigerate at least 2 hours prior to serving. Yields about 4 cups.

Pineapple Cilantro Salsa

1 c Maui pineapple, diced into 1/4 inch pieces
1 c sugar
1 c rice vinegar
2 tsp ground chili paste
1 pinch salt
1 shallot, chopped finely
2 cloves garlic, chopped finely
2 Tbl fresh cilantro, chopped

Combine all ingredients in medium saucepan and boil over medium/high heat for about 2 minutes. Cool and add cilantro. Serve at room temperature.

Yields about 1 1/2 cups.

Mild

Apricot Salsa

2/3 c fresh apricots, chopped
1/2 c red onion, chopped
1/4 c apricot preserves
1 medium red tomato, chopped
2 Tbl fresh cilantro, chopped
1 tsp ginger root, chopped finely
1/8 tsp cinnamon

Combine all ingredients and mix well. Chill until serving time. Yields about 1 cup.

Avocado and Roasted Tomatillo Salsa

1/2 lb tomatillos, roasted
1 red onion, halved
2 cloves garlic
2 Tbl fresh cilantro, chopped
1 tsp salt
1 jalapeño, seeded and chopped finely
2 small/medium avocados, peeled, pitted and chopped
2 Tbl fresh lime juice

Preheat broiler. Remove husks and rinse tomatillos under warm water to remove stickiness. Halve onion and arrange on rack of boiler with tomatillos and garlic. Broil vegetables about 8 minutes, turning once, until softened and lightly charred.

Peel garlic and place in food processor with tomatillos, 1 onion half, cilantro and salt. Remove seeds from jalapeño and chop finely. Add jalapeño to tomatillo mixture and puree until mixture is almost smooth. Transfer to a bowl.

In a smaller bowl, coat avocados in lime juice and mix well. Add avocados to tomatillo mixture, chill for 30 minutes and serve.

Yields about 11/2 cup.

Corn and Black Olive Salsa

1 1/2 c corn
2 (2 1/4 oz) cans sliced ripe olives, drained
1 red bell pepper, de-veined and chopped
1 red onion, chopped
4 garlic cloves, chopped finely
1/3 c olive oil
1/4 c fresh lemon juice
3 Tbl cider vinegar
1 tsp dried oregano
4 ripe avocados
Salt and pepper to taste

Combine corn, olives, red pepper and onion in a large bowl. In a small bowl combine garlic, oil, lemon juice, vinegar, oregano and salt and pepper to taste. Pour garlic mixture into corn mixture and mix well. Cover and refrigerate overnight. Just before serving add chopped avocados and stir into salsa. Yields about 3 cups.

Avocado Orange Salsa

3/4 c orange segments
3/4 c avocado, peeled, pitted and cut into 1/2 inch cubes
2 limes, juiced
1/4 c red onion, diced finely
1/4 c fresh cilantro, chopped finely
1 pinch dried red pepper flakes
Salt and ground black pepper to taste

Combine all ingredients and toss gently.
Refrigerate until ready to serve.
Yields about 1 1/2 cups.

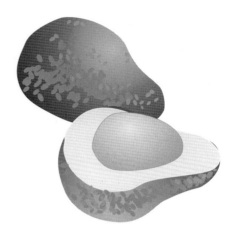

Balsamic Strawberry Salsa

1 pint strawberries, stemmed and sliced
4 tsp balsamic vinegar
1 Tbl full-bodied red wine
1 tsp sugar
1/4 tsp freshly ground black pepper

Combine all ingredients in a small glass bowl. Refrigerate until ready to serve. Yields about 1 1/2 cups.

Banana Bell Pepper Salsa

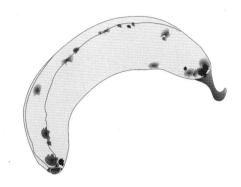

2 large bananas
1/2 c red bell pepper, de-veined, seeded and diced
1/2 c green bell pepper, de-veined, seeded and diced
1/2 c yellow bell pepper, de-veined, seeded and diced
1 Tbl ginger, minced
1/4 c fresh cilantro, chopped finely
3 Tbl lime juice
2 Tbl brown sugar, packed
 1 Tbl olive oil
Salt and pepper to taste

Combine all ingredients in a mixing bowl and gently
toss to mix. Salt, pepper, lime juice and sugar to taste.
Best served after 2 hours of refrigeration.
Yields about 2 cups.

Sweet Fruit Salsa

2 kiwis, peeled and diced
2 green apples, peeled, cored and diced
8 oz raspberries
1 lb strawberries
2 Tbl white sugar
1 Tbl brown sugar
3 Tbl fruit preserves, flavor of choice

In a large bowl thoroughly mix kiwis, apples, raspberries, strawberries, white sugar, brown sugar and fruit preserves. Cover and chill for at least 15 minutes. Best with fresh flour tortillas, buttered and lightly browned in oven or skillet or with fresh cinnamon crisps.

Yields about 3 to 4 cups.

Avocado Feta Cheese Salsa

2 plum tomatoes, chopped
1 ripe avocado, peeled, pitted and chopped
1/4 c red onion, chopped finely
1 clove garlic, minced
1 Tbl fresh parsley, chopped
1 Tbl olive oil
1 Tbl red wine vinegar
4 oz crumbled feta cheese
Freshly ground black pepper to taste

In a bowl, gently stir together tomatoes, avocados, onion and garlic. Mix in parsley and oregano. Gently stir in olive oil and vinegar. Then stir in feta. Season to taste with freshly ground black pepper. Cover and chill for 2 to 6 hours.

Yields about 1 1/2 cups.

Fruit Medley Salsa

1 Fuji apple, peeled, cored and diced
1 c fresh strawberries, sliced
2 kiwis, peeled and sliced
2 bananas, peeled and sliced
1 Tbl fresh lime juice
2 Tbl white sugar
1/2 tsp ground cinnamon
1/2 tsp ground nutmeg
Drizzle with honey

In a medium bowl mix together Fuji apple, strawberries, kiwis, bananas, lime juice, white sugar, cinnamon and nutmeg. Drizzle honey over top and then cover and refrigerate about 20 minutes before serving. Goes very well with fresh tortillas, buttered and browned in oven or skillet or with fresh cinnamon crisps.

Yields about 3 cups.

Mango Papaya Salsa

1 mango, peeled, seeded and diced
1 papaya, peeled, seeded and diced
1 large red bell pepper, seeded,
   de-veined and diced
1 ripe avocado, peeled, pitted and diced
1/2 red onion, peeled and diced
2 Tbl fresh cilantro, chopped
2 Tbl balsamic vinegar
Salt and pepper to taste

In a medium bowl, mix mango, papaya, red bell pepper, avocado, red onion, cilantro and balsamic vinegar. Season to taste with salt and pepper. Cover and chill in refrigerator at least 30 minutes prior to serving.

Yields about 2 to 3 cups.

Black Bean and Mango Salsa

1 (15oz) can black beans, rinsed and drained
1 (7oz) can whole kernel corn with peppers, drained
1 medium mango, peeled, seeded and cubed
1/4 c red onion, chopped finely
1/4 c fresh cilantro, chopped coarsely
2 Tbl fresh lime juice
1 tsp garlic salt
1/4 tsp ground cumin

In a medium bowl, combine all ingredients. Serve
with baked tortilla chips.
Yields about 3 cups.

Jalapeño Mango Salsa

1 mango, peeled, seeded and diced
1 avocado, peeled, pitted and diced
4 medium tomatoes, diced
2 jalapeño peppers, minced
1/2 c fresh cilantro, chopped
3 cloves garlic, minced
1 tsp salt
2 Tbl fresh lime juice
1/2 c red onion, chopped
3 Tbl olive oil
Black pepper to taste

In a medium bowl combine mango, avocado, tomatoes, jalapeños, cilantro and garlic. Stir in the salt, lime juice, red onion and olive oil. Black pepper to taste. Chill in a covered container for at least 30 minutes prior to serving.
Yields about 3 cups.

Jalapeño Orange Juice Salsa

4 plum tomatoes
2 large oranges, peeled and diced
1 large Vidalia onion, peeled and chopped
2 jalapeño peppers, seeded and minced
2 Tbl fresh lime juice
1/4 c fresh orange juice
1 tsp white sugar
1 Tbl fresh cilantro, chopped
Salt and ground black pepper to taste

Bring small saucepan of water to boil. Blanch tomatoes for 30 seconds and then rinse with cold water. Peel and chop tomatoes.

Place all ingredients in a large bowl and stir until mixed thoroughly. Allow to stand at room temperature for one hour. Mix and serve.

Yields about 2 to 3 cups.

Anaheim Apple Salsa

2 green apples, cored and cubed
4 Tbl fresh lime juice
2 jalapeño peppers, seeded and sliced
1 Anaheim chile, seeded and sliced
1/2 medium onion, chopped finely
2 Tbl fresh cilantro, chopped coarsely
1/2 c walnuts, lightly toasted and chopped
2 Tbl fresh ginger, peeled and thinly sliced
1/4 tsp salt

In a large bowl stir together apples and lime
juice. Stir in jalapeños and Anaheim chile
slices. Stir in onion, cilantro, walnuts, ginger
and salt. Mix thoroughly.
Refrigerate any unused salsa.
Yields about 2 cups.

Vanilla Mango Salsa

1 mango, peeled and chopped finely
1 kiwi, peeled and chopped finely
2 green onions, sliced thinly
1 jalapeño pepper, seeded and minced
1 Tbl white sugar
2 tsp fresh lime juice
1/2 tsp chili powder
1 tsp pure vanilla extract

Combine all ingredients in a medium bowl. Let stand 5 minutes for flavors to blend. Serve with grilled chicken or fish, or with fresh tortilla chips.
Yields about 1 to 2 cups.

Raspberry Sweet Onion Salsa

2 c fresh raspberries
1/4 c sweet onion, chopped
3 tsp jalapeño peppers, chopped finely
1 clove garlic, minced
1/4 c fresh cilantro, chopped
1/2 tsp white sugar
3 Tbl fresh lime juice

In a medium bowl, mix together raspberries, sweet onion, jalapeño peppers, garlic, cilantro, white sugar and lime juice. Cover and chill for at least 1 hour prior to serving.
Goes well with grilled fish or fresh tortilla chips.
Yields about 2 to 3 cups.

Watermelon Salsa

3 c chopped watermelon
1/2 c green bell pepper, chopped
2 Tbl fresh lime juice
2 Tbl fresh cilantro, chopped
1 Tbl green onions, chopped
1 Tbl jalapeño pepper, chopped
1/2 tsp garlic salt
Freshly ground black pepper to taste

In a large bowl, combine watermelon, green bell pepper, lime juice, cilantro, green onions, jalapeño, garlic salt and black pepper. Mix well and cover. Refrigerate until ready to serve.
Yields about 3 cups.

Black Bean and Cantaloupe Salsa

1 c black beans, cooked and drained
1 very ripe cantaloupe, peeled and diced
1/2 red bell pepper, de-veined, seeded and diced
1/2 green bell pepper, de-veined, seeded and diced
3/4 c canned pineapple juice
1/2 red onion, sliced thinly
1/2 c fresh lime juice
1/2 c fresh cilantro, chopped finely
1 Tbl ground cumin
Salt and freshly ground black pepper to taste

Combine all ingredients in a large bowl and cover.
Refrigerate for at least 1 hour prior to serving.
Yields about 3 cups.

Guacamole

The Avocado

The avocado began its distinguished history sometime between 7,000 B.C. and 5,000 B.C. in south-central Mexico. Archaeologists in Peru have found domesticated avocado seeds buried with Incan mummies dating back to 750 B.C.

Avocados took their name from Spanish conquistadors who adored their taste but could not pronounce the difficult Aztec name. They changed it to aguacate, which eventually evolved into avocado in English.

Today 95 percent of the U.S. crop of avocados is grown in California. According to the California Avocado Commission, most California avocados are harvested on 60,000 acres between San Luis Obispo and the Mexican border.

There are seven varieties of avocados grown commercially in California, Haas being the most popular. They are as follows:

- Bacon is a mid-winter green variety, available late fall into early spring. It is oval shaped with smooth, thin green skin, a medium- to large-seed and a light taste.
- Fuerte is harvested late fall through spring. It is pear-shaped with thin, smooth green skin, a medium seed and pale green flesh.
- Gwen is a Haas-like green variety but slightly larger. It has pebbly-thick green skin, a small- to medium-seed and creamy, gold-green flesh. Green skin turns dull when ripe.
- Haas is distinctive with green skin that becomes purplish-black when it becomes ripe. It has pebbly-thick, but pliant skin, a small- to medium-seed and pale green flesh with a creamy texture.
- Pinkerton avocados have small seeds and yield more fruit per tree. They are a long pear-shaped fruit with medium-thick green skin with slight pebbling and creamy pale green flesh. Its green skin deepens in color as it ripens.
- Reed is a large round fruit available in the summer months and early fall. It has thick, green skin with slight pebbling, a medium seed and buttery flesh. Skin remains green when ripened.
- Zutano is recognized for its shiny, yellow-green skin. It is one of the first varieties harvested when the season begins in September and is available through early winter. It is pear-shaped with an average to large size. Its flesh is pale green with a light texture. Its skin retains yellow-green color when ripened.

Hot

Roasted Corn Guacamole

4 ripe avocados, peeled, pitted and mashed
1 c roasted corn kernels
1/4 c fresh lime juice
1 medium red Roma tomato, seeded and diced
4 cloves garlic, chopped finely
3 jalapeño peppers, chopped finely with seeds
1 tsp ground cumin
Salt and freshly ground black pepper to taste

In a medium bowl, coarsely mash avocados.
Fold in remaining ingredients. Squeeze lime
juice into avocado mixture and serve.

Yields about 2 cups.

Serrano Mango Guacamole

2 ripe avocados, peeled, pitted and coarsely mashed
1 ripe mango, chopped
1/2 red onion, chopped
1 medium red tomato, seeded and diced
1 clove garlic, minced
2 Serrano chilies, seeded and chopped
2 Tbl fresh cilantro, chopped
2 Tbl fresh lime juice
1 Tbl low fat sour cream
Salt and freshly ground black pepper to taste

Combine all ingredients and chill at least 1 hour to let flavors mix.

Yields about 2 cups.

Blackened Tomatillo Guacamole

12 medium tomatillos, husked and rinsed
1/2 c white onion, chopped finely
1/2 c red onion, chopped finely
1/2 c fresh cilantro, chopped coarsely
4 Serrano chilies, seeded and minced
2 Tbl fresh lime juice
3 large ripe avocados, peeled, pitted and coarsely mashed
Salt and freshly ground black pepper to taste

Preheat broiler. Line rimmed baking sheet with aluminum foil. Place tomatillos on prepared baking sheet. Broil until tomatillos are just blackened in spots and tender, about 8 minutes each side.

Combine onions, cilantro, chilies and lime juice in large bowl. Add roasted tomatillos and any juices from baking sheet to onion mixture. Using fork mash coarsely. Add avocados and mash with fork until mixture is very coarsely pureed and some chunks remain. Season to taste with salt and freshly ground black pepper. Yields 3 to 4 cups.

Plum Poblano Guacamole

3 Poblano chilies
1 large jalapeño pepper
8 Tbl fresh lime juice
1 large plum tomato, seeded and chopped
2 small green onions, chopped finely
1 tsp grated lime peel
Salt to taste
2 large ripe avocados, peeled,
    pitted and coarsely mashed
2/3 c red onion, chopped finely
1/2 c fresh cilantro, chopped coarsely
1/4 tsp ground cumin

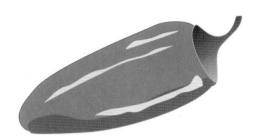

Char Poblano and jalapeño chilies directly over gas flame or under broiler until blackened on all sides. Enclose in a paper or plastic bag at least ten minutes or until skins are loosened. Peel, seed and finely chop chilies. Mix chilies, 1 tablespoon lime juice, tomato, green onions and lime peel in small bowl. Season with salt.

Puree avocados, 7 tablespoons lime juice, red onion, cilantro and cumin in processor until almost smooth. Season with salt.

Cover each mixture separately and refrigerate until ready to serve.

When serving, spoon avocado puree into wide shallow bowl. Spoon chili mixture into center.

Yields about 2 cups.

Mint and White Onion Guacamole

4 ripe avocados, peeled, pitted and mashed
2 Tbl fresh lemon juice
1 Tbl honey
1 large plum tomato, diced finely
1/2 c white onion, chopped finely
1/2 c fresh cilantro, chopped finely
1/4 c fresh mint, chopped finely
3 Tbl Serrano peppers, chopped finely
Salt and freshly ground black pepper to taste

In a medium/large bowl, coarsely mash avocados. Stir in lemon juice and honey. Fold in remaining ingredients. Serve immediately. Yields about 3 cups.

Spicy Fruit Guacamole

1/3 c white onions, chopped finely
3 Serrano chilies, chopped finely
1 tsp coarse salt
4 large ripe avocados, peeled, pitted and coarsely mashed
3 Tbl fresh lime juice
3/4 c pear, peeled and diced finely
3/4 c seedless grapes, halved
3/4 c pomegranate seeds
2 Tbl honey
Freshly ground black pepper to taste

Process onions, chilies and salt into a rough paste. Gradually add avocado, coarsely mashing it, leaving chunks. Stir in the lemon juice. In a separate bowl mix the pear, grapes and 1/2 cup of pomegranate seeds with honey and black pepper to taste. Combine fruits with avocados, mix and then sprinkle remaining pomegranate seeds over guacamole. Chill until ready to serve.

Yields about 3 cups.

Banana Pepper Guacamole

5 ripe avocados, peeled, pitted and coarsely mashed
2 red tomatoes, chopped
1 bunch green onions, chopped
1/4 c hot banana peppers, chopped
3 jalapeño peppers, minced
2 garlic cloves, minced
3 Tbl fresh cilantro, chopped
1/4 c fresh lime juice
Salt and freshly ground black pepper to taste

Coarsely mash avocados in large bowl. Add tomato, green onions, banana peppers, jalapeño peppers, garlic cilantro and fresh lime juice. Salt and ground pepper to taste and mix all ingredients well. Serve immediately.
Yields about 4 cups.

Hot Pepper and Tofu Guacamole

2 large ripe avocados, peeled,
  pitted and mashed
1/2 c tofu
1/2 small white onion, minced
1 clove garlic, minced
1 Tbl lemon juice
1 tsp Worcestershire sauce
6 drops hot pepper sauce
1 tsp salt
1/2 plum tomato, diced
1 Serrano chili, minced
1 Tbl fresh cilantro, chopped

Mix tofu in blender until smooth. Coarsely
mash avocados in a medium bowl and then
add tofu. Fold in all other ingredients, chill
and serve.
Yields about 2 cups.

Serrano Green Tomato Guacamole

3 medium ripe avocados, peeled, pitted and mashed
1/4 c fresh lime juice
9 green tomatoes, peeled
12 small Serrano chilies
2 cloves garlic, chopped
3 Tbl fresh cilantro, chopped coarsely
2 c water
Salt and freshly ground black pepper to taste

Place water in one-quart saucepan and bring to boil. Add green tomatoes and chilies. Boil for about 10 seconds only and remove. In a blender, combine tomatoes, chilies and chopped garlic. Mix well.
Coarsely mash avocados in medium bowl and mix with lime juice. Add blended mixture and then cilantro.
Serve immediately.
Yields about 3 cups.

Cranberry Guacamole

2 ripe avocados, peeled, pitted and coarsely mashed
1 (7oz) can salsa verde
3 Tbl fresh cilantro, chopped coarsely
1 Tbl fresh lemon juice
1 Tbl fresh orange juice
3 tsp jalapeño peppers, chopped finely
1 tsp coarse garlic salt
1/2 c dried cranberries
1 Tbl white onion, finely chopped
White pepper to taste

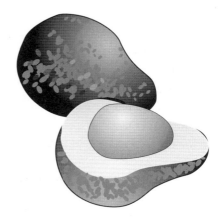

In a medium bowl, coarsely mash avocados and add salsa verde, cilantro, lemon juice, orange juice, jalapeño and garlic salt. Mix well. Fold in cranberries and onion. Season to taste with white pepper.

Serve with tortilla chips or sliced vegetables.

Yields about 2 cups.

Boiled Tomatillo Guacamole

8 tomatillos, husked and boiled
1 Tbl salt
1/2 c fresh cilantro, chopped coarsely
1/2 c white onion, minced
3 jalapeño, minced finely
4 ripe avocados, peeled, pitted and coarsely mashed
1 Tbl low-fat sour cream
Salt and freshly ground black pepper to taste

Over medium heat, bring 2 quarts water to boil. Stir in salt and add husked tomatillos. Cook for about 10 minutes and then remove. Place cooked tomatillos in blender and puree until smooth. Set mixture aside. In a medium-mixing bowl, coarsely mash avocados. Stir in cooled tomatillo puree and add the remaining ingredients. Salt and black pepper to taste. Cover tightly with plastic wrap and refrigerate until ready to serve. Yields about 2 to 3 cups.

Red Pepper Crab Guacamole

2 ripe avocados, peeled, pitted and coarsely mashed
1 tsp grated lime peel
1 Tbl fresh lime juice
10 drops red pepper sauce
1/2 tsp garlic salt
1 (6oz) can crab, rinsed and picked through for shells
2 Tbl green onion, chopped
3 Tbl capers, rinsed

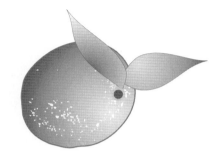

In a medium bowl combine coarsely mashed avocados, lime peel and juice, red pepper sauce and garlic salt. Stir in crab, green onion and capers.
Serve with tortilla chips. Yields about 2 cups.

Shrimp Guacamole

2 ripe avocados, peeled, pitted and coarsely mashed
1 tsp grated lime peel
1 Tbl fresh lime juice
10 drops red pepper sauce
1/2 tsp coarse garlic salt
4 oz cooked, shelled and de-veined small shrimp
2 Tbl fresh dill, chopped
1 medium leek (white to light green parts only), chopped finely

In a medium bowl combine coarsely mashed avocados, lime peel and juice, red pepper sauce and garlic salt.
Coarsely chop shrimp.
Stir in shrimp, dill and leek.
Serve with tortilla chips or fresh cut vegetables.
Yields about 2 cups.

Roasted Poblano Chili Guacamole

7 ripe avocados, peeled, pitted
   and coarsely mashed
1/2 c fresh cilantro, chopped coarsely
1/2 c tomato, chopped
1/2 c red onion, chopped
2 Tbl fresh lime juice
1 tsp cumin
1 tsp chili powder
2 roasted Poblano chilies, chopped
1 Tbl garlic, minced
Salt and freshly ground black pepper to taste

Heat broiler. Slice Poblano chilies in half and place in broiler for about 2 to 3 minutes, until lightly browned. Remove and chop.

In a large mixing bowl, coarsely mash avocados, leaving some chunks. Add remaining ingredients into avocado bowl and mix. Season to taste with salt and pepper.

Serve immediately with tortilla chips.

Yields about 3 to 4 cups.

Guacamole Autentico

4 ripe California Avocados, peeled and seeded
1 tsp ground cumin
1 ripe, medium Roma tomato, seeded and diced
1/2 c sweet white onion, minced
2 Serrano chilies, seeded and minced
1/4 c fresh cilantro, chopped
4 Tbl fresh lime juice
Hot pepper sauce, sea salt and white pepper to taste

Cut avocado in large chunks and mash coarsely in large bowl with fork. Add remaining ingredients and blend gently, leaving some small chunks. Season to taste with pepper sauce, salt and white pepper.

This recipe is courtesy of the California Avocado Commission.

Jalapeño Honey Guacamole

4 ripe avocados, peeled, pitted
   and coarsely mashed
2 Tbl fresh lemon juice
1 Tbl honey
1/2 c white onion, chopped finely
1/2 c fresh cilantro, chopped finely
1/2 c fresh mint, chopped finely
3 Tbl jalapeño pepper, chopped finely
1 tsp salt
Freshly ground black pepper to taste.

Coarsely mash avocados, leaving some chunks
and stir in lemon juice and honey. Fold in
remaining ingredients and then season with
black pepper to taste.
Serve immediately.

Yields about 2 to 3 cups.

Serrano Tomatillo Guacamole

2 small white onions, diced
12 small Serrano chilies, stemmed, seeded and finely chopped
1 large bunch fresh cilantro, chopped
1 1/2 tsp coarse salt
24 medium tomatillos, husked, washed and roasted
1 tsp freshly ground black pepper
8 ripe avocados, peeled, pitted and coarsely mashed

Preheat broiler. Remove tomatillo husks and rinse under warm water. Place tomatillos in broiler and heat for about 8 minutes or until lightly charred. Set aside.
In a large bowl combine onion, chilies, cilantro and salt. Add the tomatillos a few at a time, mashing and blending with a fork to a fine paste. Add the avocado and mash until it is thick and chunky. Salt and black pepper to taste.
Serve with sliced tomato and chips.

Yields about 4 to 6 cups.

Avocado Preparation and Tips

To tell if an avocado is ripe, gently squeeze. A ripe avocado will yield to gentle pressure, but still remain firm.

- Do not go by color to estimate ripeness. Some varieties retain their light color even when ripe.
- Avoid fruit with dark blemishes on the skin.
- To ripen an avocado, place the fruit in a plain brown paper bag. Including an apple or banana will speed the process because they release ethylene gas, a ripening reagent.
- To peel an avocado simply slice the fruit lengthwise, remove seed with a spoon and then use spoon to scoop out the insides.
- Lemon juice, lime juice, white vinegar or the seed itself help to prevent browning.
- To store cut fruit, sprinkle it with lemon juice, lime juice or white vinegar. Place in an airtight container and refrigerate for no more than two to three days.

Avocados can be frozen for storage but must be peeled, sliced and covered in lemon juice, lime juice or white vinegar. Place in an airtight container with about an inch of air space between the avocados and the lid. Freeze and use within 4 to 5 months.

Medium

Monterey Jack Guacamole

15 ripe avocados, peeled, pitted and coarsely mashed
1 large red onion, chopped
3 garlic cloves, chopped
3 tomatoes, diced
1/2 lb Monterey Jack cheese, grated
5 green chilies, diced
5 jalapeño peppers, de-veined, seeded and chopped finely
1 c fresh cilantro, chopped
1/2 c fresh lime juice
 Salt and freshly ground black pepper to taste

In a large mixing bowl, coarsely mash avocados, leaving some chunks. Add remaining ingredients and mix.
Serve with tortilla chips or fresh vegetables.
Yields about 6 to 8 cups.

Rich and Creamy Guacamole

15 ripe medium California avocados,
    peeled and seeded
4 cloves garlic, crushed
1/3 c fresh lemon juice
1/2 c fresh cilantro, chopped
1 Tbl salt
1/2 c sour cream
1/2 c low-fat mayonnaise
2 tsp Tabasco sauce

In a large mixing bowl coarsely mash avocados, leaving some chunks. Add remaining ingredients and mix to blend.

This recipe is courtesy of the California Avocado Commission.

Salsa Fresca Guacamole

2c plum tomatoes, chopped finely
1 c white onion, chopped finely
1/4 c fresh cilantro, chopped coarsely
3 Ancho chilies, de-veined, seeded and chopped
1 clove garlic, minced
2 limes, juiced
1/2 c vegetable broth
Salt and pepper to taste

4 ripe avocados, peeled, pitted and coarsely mashed
2 limes, juiced
Salt and pepper to taste

To make red salsa fresca, mix chopped onion, cilantro, chilies, garlic, lime juice and vegetable broth in a medium bowl. Season to taste with salt and ground black pepper and mix well.

In another bowl, coarsely mash avocados with lime juice and then salt and pepper to taste. Mix salsa fresca with mashed avocados. Serve immediately with fresh tortilla chips.

Yields about 3 to 4 cups.

Cherry Tomato Guacamole

2 large avocados, peeled,
   pitted and coarsely ground
2Tbl fresh lemon juice
1/2 c red bell pepper, diced finely
1/2 c cherry tomatoes, halved
1/4 c green onions, sliced thinly
1/2 red onion, chopped finely
3 cloves garlic, chopped finely
1/2 tsp fresh thyme, chopped
1/2 tsp salt
1/4 tsp freshly ground black pepper
1/4 tsp cayenne pepper
1 Tbl fresh cilantro, chopped

Coarsely mash avocados, leaving chunks and then stir in lemon juice. Fold in remaining ingredients.
Serve immediately.

Yields about 2 to 3 cups.

Tomatillo Hot Pepper Guacamole

3 ripe avocados, peeled, pitted
   and coarsely mashed
3 tomatillos, husked and chopped
1 red onion, chopped finely
3 plum tomatoes, seeded and chopped
1 Tbl fresh lime juice
1 tsp red pepper flakes
Hot pepper sauce to taste
Salt and freshly ground black pepper to taste

In a medium bowl mix avocados, tomatillos, red onion, roma tomatoes and lime juice. Season with red pepper flakes, hot pepper sauce, salt and ground black pepper. Cover and refrigerate at least 45 minutes before serving.

Yields about 3 to 4 cups.

Cream Cheese Salsa Guacamole

3 ripe avocados, peeled, pitted and coarsely mashed
1 Tbl low-fat sour cream
2 (3oz) packages low-fat cream cheese, softened
2 Tbl salsa of choice (see salsa recipes)
1/2 c red onion, chopped finely
Salt and ground black pepper to taste

In a small bowl mix together avocados, sour cream, cream cheese, salsa and onion. Season with salt and ground black pepper and then blend to desired consistency. Refrigerate until ready to serve.

Yields about 3 cups.

Anaheim Asparagus Guacamole

1 medium Anaheim chili
1 tsp olive oil
5 fresh asparagus spears, ends trimmed
1/2 c nonfat plain yogurt
2 medium avocados, peeled, pitted and cubed
1 plum tomato, seeded and diced
1 Tbl green onion, chopped
1/4 c fresh cilantro, chopped
1 Tbl fresh lime juice
Dash of garlic powder
1/2 tsp salt
1/2 tsp freshly ground black pepper

Preheat broiler. Wearing rubber gloves to protect skin, rub chile with oil and then broil for 5 minutes. Turn chile with tongs so all sides are equally charred. Transfer chile to a plastic bag, seal and let steam for about 10 minutes or until skin is loosened. Remove stem, skin and seeds from chili and dice. Set aside.

Fill medium sauté pan halfway with water and bring to a boil. Prepare a medium-sized bowl of ice water. Place asparagus spears into boiling water for 3 to 4 minutes or until just tender. Remove and plunge spears into icy water to halt cooking and preserve color. When cool, remove, dry thoroughly and chop into 1-inch pieces. Transfer to blender or food processor, add yogurt and avocado and process until smooth.

Transfer to a mixing bowl and stir remaining ingredients into mix. Serve with fresh tortilla chips.

Yields about 3 cups.

Goat Cheese Guacamole

2 ripe avocados, peeled,
   pitted and coarsely mashed
1/2 c fresh white goat cheese,
   crumbled finely and chilled
1/4 c fresh cilantro, chopped
2 Tbl toasted pistachio nuts, chopped
1/2 tsp crushed red pepper flakes
2 large garlic cloves, chopped finely
1/2 large red onion, chopped finely

Coarsely mash avocados, leaving chunks. Fold
in remaining ingredients. Serve immediately
with tortilla chips.
Yields about 2 to 3 cups.

Caribbean Guacamole

2 ripe avocados, peeled, pitted and coarsely mashed
1/2 Tbl fresh lime juice
1/2 c fresh mango, seeded and diced finely
1/2 pineapple, peeled, pitted and diced finely
2 Tbl dried shredded unsweetened coconut
1/2 tsp crushed red pepper flakes
2 Tbl fresh cilantro, chopped finely
Salt and freshly ground black pepper to taste

Coarsely mash avocados, leaving chunks. Stir in lime juice and then fold in remaining ingredients.
Serve immediately with tortilla chips.

This recipe is courtesy of the California Avocado Commission.

Citrus Guacamole

3 ripe avocados, peeled, pitted and coarsely mashed
3 tomatoes, peeled, seeded and diced
1/4 c red onion, minced
1 lime, juiced and grated rind
2 Tbl fresh lemon juice
2 Tbl fresh orange juice
1/2 tsp coarse salt
1/4 c low-fat mayonnaise
1/4 c low-fat sour cream
3 dashes hot pepper sauce

Combine all ingredients and serve immediately with tortilla chips.

Yields about 3 cups.

Anaheim Corn Guacamole

1 c corn kernels
2 Anaheim chilies, chopped
1/4 red onion, chopped
1 Tbl olive oil
2 ripe avocados, peeled,
    pitted and mashed coarsely
4 Tbl fresh lime juice
2 Tbl medium/hot salsa
1/4 c fresh cilantro, chopped
2 tsp salt
1/2 tsp freshly ground black pepper
Dash of hot pepper sauce

Preheat oven to 450 degrees and line a baking sheet with foil. Coat foil with cooking spray.

Toss corn, whole chilies and chopped onion with oil in large boil and mix. Spread in single layer on prepared baking sheet.

Roast for 15-20 minutes until vegetables are lightly browned.

When cool, peel chilies and chop finely. Set aside corn, chilies and onion mixture and let cool.

In a large mixing bowl coarsely mash avocados and then mix with lime juice. Stir in corn mixture and add salsa and cilantro. Season with salt, pepper and hot pepper sauce.

Serve with tortilla chips.

Yields about 3 cups.

Green Chili Tofu Guacamole

4 ripe avocados, peeled,
   pitted and mashed coarsely
1 (10 1/2 oz) pack of tofu, drained
1/4 red onion, chopped
1 1/2 Tbl plain yogurt
2 cloves garlic, pressed
1 tsp Tabasco sauce
1 tsp salt
Garnish with sliced red bell pepper

Drain excess water from tofu and combine
with plain yogurt in a small bowl. Mash with
a fork. In a large bowl, coarsely mash avocados, leaving chunks. Mix tofu and yogurt in
with avocados and add pressed garlic, Tabasco
sauce and salt. Mix well and garnish with
thinly sliced red bell pepper.
Serve with tortilla chips or fresh vegetables.
Yields about 4 cups.

Pistachio Guacamole

4 ripe avocados, peeled, pitted and coarsely mashed
2 Tbl fresh lime juice
1 c white goat cheese, fresh and crumbled finely
1/2 c fresh cilantro, chopped
1/4 c pistachio nuts, chopped and toasted
1/2 tsp red pepper flakes, crushed
4 cloves garlic, chopped finely

Coarsely mash avocados in a medium bowl. Fold in remaining ingredients. Serve with tortilla chips for fresh vegetables.
Yields about 3 cups.

Sweet Onion Guacamole

4 ripe avocados, peeled,
   pitted and coarsely mashed
4 Tbl low-fat plain yogurt
1/2 c red onion, chopped finely
1/2 c yellow onion, chopped finely
4 cloves garlic, minced
4 Tbl fresh cilantro, chopped finely
1 Chile de Arbol, dried and finely crushed
1 tsp cumin powder
1/2 tsp salt
1/2 tsp pepper
2 Tbl fresh lime juice

In a medium bowl coarsely mash avocados, leaving chunks. Combine all remaining ingredients, cover and refrigerate for about 1 hour before serving.
Serve with tortilla chips.

Yields about 4 cups.

Yogurt Dill Guacamole

15 ripe medium avocados, peeled, pitted and coarsely mashed
1/4 c fresh lemon juice
3 Tbl fresh dill, chopped
2 Tbl fresh cilantro, chopped
1 1/2 Tbl garlic salt
1/2 c medium/hot salsa (see salsa recipes)
3 c low-fat plain yogurt

In a large mixing bowl coarsely mash avocados, leaving some chunks. Add all remaining ingredients and mix well.
Serve immediately with fresh tortilla chips.
Yields about 6 to 7 cups.

Green Salsa Guacamole

2 ripe avocados, peeled,
   pitted and coarsely mashed
1/4 c salsa verde
1 1/4 tsp grated lemon peel
1 Tbl fresh lemon juice
1 tsp coarse garlic salt
3 Tbl red bell pepper, chopped finely
3 Tbl fresh basil leaves, chopped
1 medium shallot, chopped finely

In a medium bowl combine avocados, salsa,
lemon peel and juice and garlic salt. Stir in
bell pepper, basil and shallot.
Serve with tortilla chips or fresh vegetables.
Yields about 2 to 3 cups.

Black Bean Pepper Guacamole

2 ripe avocados, peeled, pitted and coarsely mashed
1 Tbl fresh lemon juice
2 cloves garlic, chopped finely
1/2 tsp salt
1/2 c black beans, rinsed and drained
3 Tbl red onion, chopped
 3 Tbl tomato, chopped
2 pickled jalapeños, chopped
Freshly ground black pepper to taste.

In a medium bowl combine avocados, lemon juice, garlic and salt. Stir in beans, onion, tomato and jalapeño. Season to taste with freshly ground black pepper.
Serve with fresh tortilla chips.

Yields about 3 cups.

Japanese Guacamole

1 (6oz) Daikon (Japanese radish), shredded
1 tsp salt
4 California avocados
2 oz green onion, sliced finely
1/2 c fresh salmon caviar
1/2 c rice vinegar (plain)
2 Tbl Japanese soy sauce
1 Tbl Wasabi paste

Toss daikon with salt; drain in a colander for half an hour. Squeeze out as much liquid as possible; reserve.
Coarsely mash California avocados. Fold in remaining ingredients and reserved daikon.
Serve with rice crackers, shrimp chips.

This recipe is courtesy of the California Avocado Commission.

Spanish Guacamole

4 California avocados
1 c green onions, chopped coarsely
1/2 c coarsely chopped, toasted, slivered almonds
4 large cloves garlic, chopped finely
1 jalapeño pepper, chopped finely
1/4 c medium-dry sherry
2 Tbl parsley, chopped finely
Salt to taste, depending on the saltiness of the olives

Coarsely mash California avocados, leaving chunks. Fold in remaining ingredients.

This recipe is courtesy of the California Avocado Commission.

Yellow Pepper Guacamole

2 ripe avocados, peeled,
   pitted and coarsely mashed
3 Tbl fresh lemon juice
3 Tbl tomato, chopped
2 Tbl yellow bell pepper, chopped
1/2 tsp salt
2 Tbl fresh cilantro, chopped
1 pickled jalapeño pepper, chopped finely

Coarsely mash avocados in a medium bowl.
Mix well with lemon juice. Add all remaining
ingredients and mix well.
Serve immediately with fresh tortilla chips.

Yields about 3 cups.

Mild

Basic Guacamole

2 ripe avocados, peeled, pitted and coarsely mashed
1 large ripe tomato, diced
1/4 c red onion, finely chopped
2 cloves garlic, minced
3 Tbl fresh cilantro, chopped finely
1 large lime, juiced
1/2 tsp ground cumin
 Salt and freshly ground black pepper to taste

In a medium bowl coarsely mash avocados, leaving some chunks. Add all remaining ingredients and mix well.
Serve immediately with fresh tortilla chips.

Yields about 3 cups.

Cajun Guacamole

2 California avocados
1 Tbl fresh lemon juice
1/2 c red bell pepper, diced finely
1/2 c small cherry tomatoes,
   cut in halves or quarters if large
1/2 c green onions, sliced thinly
3 cloves garlic, chopped finely
1/2 tsp fresh thyme leaves, chopped
1/2 tsp salt
1/4 tsp freshly ground black pepper
1/8 tsp cayenne pepper

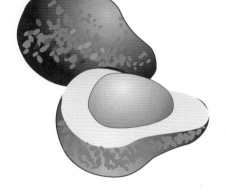

Coarsely mash avocados; stir in lemon juice. Fold in remaining ingredients.

This recipe is courtesy of the California Avocado Commission.

Balsamic Roasted Onion Guacamole

1 large purple onion, chopped
2 cloves garlic, chopped
2 Tbl balsamic vinegar
1 Tbl olive oil
4 small California avocados, peeled
1 Tbl lemon juice
1/2 tsp salt
1/2 tsp dried Italian seasoning

Preheat oven to 425 degrees F.
Toss together first 4 ingredients. Place in an aluminum foil lined baking pan. Bake for 25 to 30 minutes or until lightly browned, stirring once. Allow to cool.
Mash avocados in a medium bowl. Stir in onion mixture, lemon juice, salt and Italian seasoning. Chill for 1 hour before serving.

This recipe is courtesy of the California Avocado Commission.

Argentinean Guacamole

Large pinch of saffron threads
4 California avocados
2 Tbl fresh lemon juice
1/2 c white onion, chopped finely
1/4 c fresh parsley, chopped
2 tsp fresh thyme leaves, chopped
4 large cloves garlic
1 tsp salt

Lightly toast saffron threads in a dry frying pan (Take care not to burn).
Pulverize in a mortar and pestle and set aside. Coarsely mash California avocados. Fold in remaining ingredients, including saffron. Serve with purple potato and sweet potato chips.

This recipe is courtesy of the California Avocado Commission.

Sesame Seed Guacamole

1 Tbl white sesame seed
1 large ripe avocado, peeled, pitted and coarsely mashed
1 Tbl pickled ginger, shredded
3 Tbl rice vinegar
1/2 tsp Wasabi powder

Place sesame seeds in skillet over medium/high heat. Shake pan often until seeds begins to pop or 3 to 4 minutes. Pour from pan into small bowl and set aside to cool.

In a medium bowl mix avocado, 1/2 teaspoon sesame seed, ginger, vinegar and wasabi. Mix gently.

Transfer to a serving bowl and sprinkle with remaining seeds. Serve with potsticker crisps.

Yields about 1 1/2 cups.

Garbanzo Guacamole

1 can garbanzo beans, drained and rinsed
1 Tbl fresh lemon juice
1 clove garlic, crushed
1 medium red onion, chopped
1 ripe avocado, peeled, pitted and chopped
1 medium red tomato, chopped
4 scallions, thinly sliced
1 Tbl green chilies, chopped

Place garbanzo beans in a food processor or blender. Add lemon juice and garlic and process until garbanzos are slightly chopped, about 30 seconds. Add onion and avocado and mix again, leaving mixture chunky. Place mixture in a bowl and add remaining ingredients. Mix well, cover and chill for 1 hour before serving.

Yields about 2 cups.

Tofu Guacamole

1 ripe avocado, peeled, pitted and coarsely mashed
1/8 lb Tofu, firm style
1 lemon, juiced
3 cloves garlic, minced
1/2 red bell pepper, chopped
2 green onions, chopped finely
2 Tbl fresh parsley, chopped
1/2 tsp curry powder
1/2 tsp oregano
1/2 tsp thyme
1/4 tsp freshly ground black pepper
4 Tbl hot pepper sauce

Mash avocado and tofu in a medium bowl. Juice lemon over the top and mix well. Add garlic, bell pepper, green onion and all spices and mix well. Hot pepper sauce to taste. Refrigerate for 1 hour before serving.
Yields about 2 to 3 cups.

Green Chile Guacamole

4 large ripe avocados, peeled,
    pitted and coarsely mashed
1/2 c red onion, chopped finely
1/2 c plum tomatoes, seeded and chopped
1/2 c fresh cilantro, chopped
1 (4oz) can diced green chilies, drained
2 tsp jalapeño peppers, chopped finely
Salt and freshly ground black pepper to taste

Coarsely mash avocados in a large bowl. Mix in
onion, tomatoes, cilantro and canned chilies. Add
jalapeños to taste. Salt and freshly ground black
pepper to taste. Refrigerate until ready to serve.
Yields about 3 cups.

Vermouth Guacamole

2 ripe avocados, peeled, pitted and coarsely mashed
1/2 Tbl fresh lime juice
2 Tbl shallot, chopped finely
1 1/2 Tbl dry vermouth
1 Tbl fresh tarragon, chopped
1/2 tsp salt

In a medium bowl coarsely mash avocados, leaving some chunks. Stir in lime juice.
Fold in remaining ingredients.
Serve immediately with fresh tortilla chips or vegetables.

This recipe is courtesy of the California Avocado Commission.

Greek Guacamole

2 ripe avocados, peeled, pitted and coarsely mashed
1 Tbl fresh lemon juice
1/4 c small cherry tomatoes, halved
1/3 c cucumber, peeled and diced finely
1/4 c red onion, chopped finely
1/4 c Kalamata olives, pitted and chopped
1/4 cup Feta cheese, finely crumbled
1 tsp fresh marjoram, chopped

Coarsely mash avocados and stir in lemon juice. Fold in all remaining ingredients. Serve immediately with fresh tortilla chips or with whole wheat crackers.

This recipe is courtesy of the California Avocado Commission.

Italian Parmesan Guacamole

2 ripe avocados, peeled, pitted and coarsely mashed
1/2 Tbl white wine vinegar
1 Tbl fresh basil leaves, shredded
3 Tbl grated Parmesan cheese
2 Tbl sun-dried tomato (packed in oil), drained, chopped
2 Tbl toasted pine nuts
Salt and freshly ground black pepper to taste.

In a medium bowl coarsely mash avocados, leaving some chunks. Stir in vinegar. Fold in remaining ingredients.
Serve immediately with fresh tortilla chips.

This recipe is courtesy of the California Avocado Commission.

Blue Cheese Guacamole

6 ripe medium avocados, peeled,
   pitted and coarsely mashed
1 Tbl fresh lime juice
10 drops red pepper sauce
1/2 tsp coarse garlic salt
1/4 c crumbled blue cheese
3 Tbl red bell pepper, chopped finely
1 large red tomato, diced
2 Tbl fresh Italian parsley leaves, chopped finely

In a medium bowl combine avocados, lime
juice, red pepper sauce and garlic salt. Mix well.
Stir in blue cheese, bell pepper, tomato and
parsley.
Serve with tortilla chips or cut vegetables.
Yields about 4 cups.

Italian Seasoned Guacamole

1 large red onion, chopped
2 cloves garlic, chopped
2 Tbl balsamic vinegar
1 Tbl olive oil
4 ripe avocados, peeled, pitted and coarsely mashed
 1 Tbl fresh lemon juice
1/2 tsp salt
1/2 tsp dried Italian seasoning

Toss together first 4 ingredients. Place in an aluminum foil-lined baking pan. Bake at 425 degrees F for 25 to 30 minutes or until lightly browned, stirring once. Set aside and cool.

In a medium bowl, coarsely mash avocados, leaving chunks. Stir in onion mixture, lemon juice, salt and Italian seasoning.

Cover and refrigerate for 1 hour prior to serving.

Serve with tortilla chips.

Yields about 3 cups.

Get the freshest avocados around by growing your own! Here are some tips from the California Avocado Commission:

Avocado trees like a soil ph of 6 to 6.5.

- These are shallow-rooted trees that like good aeration.
- They do best with a woody mulch about 2" in diameter. Use about 1/3 cubic yard per tree but keep it about 6 to 8 inches away from the trunk.
- Take care not to disturb the delicate root system when planting. If the ball is root-bound, carefully loosen the soil around the edge and clip any roots that are going in circles.
- The ideal time to plant is March through June. During the summer there is a risk of sun damage and the young trees may not take up enough water.
- The hole should be as deep as the root ball and just a bit wider.
- Once gently planted, fill the hole with soil. Do not use gravel or potting mix.
- The major nutrients needed by avocado trees are Nitrogen, Phosphorus and Potassium (NPK) in a 7-4-2 fertilizer and Zinc.
- Feed young trees 1/2 to 1 pound of actual nitrogen per tree per year.
- When watering, soak the soil as well and then allow it to dry somewhat before watering again.
- Typically trees need to be watered two to three times a week. A mature tree will take about 20 gallons of water a day.

This information was provided by Dr. Mary Lu Arpaia, Extension Subtropical Horticulturist, Kearny Agriculture Center, Parlier, CA and Dr. Ben Faber, Farm Advisor, Soils and Water, Avocados and Subtropicals, Ventura County, CA

California Avocado Commission

"The California Avocado Commission was created to cost-effectively build value for the California avocado brand through demand-building programs including advertising, merchandising, foodservice, public relations and nutrition." They have been very successful in their endeavor and the value and demand of their healthy, tasty product continues to grow at an increasingly fast rate.

The newly-updated Food Pyramid from the United States Department of Agriculture (USDA), now titled MyPyramid proves yet again the importance of fruits and vegetables by visually communicating that they should be consumed more regularly than any other food group. Avocados are featured on the MyPyramid website and are listed as a healthy fruit choice.

The California Avocado Commission website, www.avocado.org contends that the avocado, on top of providing excellent health and nutrient benefits, can also be used to prevent weight gain and/or maintain a healthy weight. Here are just a few reasons:

- Like other fruits and vegetables, avocados provide satiety because of their water and fiber content. This increases the feeling of fullness and can be used as part of an effective weight loss/weight management plan.
- Naturally cholesterol-free, avocados are a delicious and nutritious alternative to saturated fat-laden spreads, toppings and dips.

Choosing a California Avocado increases the intake of vitamins, minerals, fiber and other key nutrients, especially those that are often lacking in typical diets.

Avocados have also been found to lower chronic disease risks by lowering intake of saturated fats, trans fats, cholesterol and sodium. The California Avocado Commission contends that:

- Avocados offer mono unsaturated fat, which supports heart health.
- Avocados are sodium- and cholesterol-free and like other fruits and vegetables, avocados offer several vitamins, minerals and phytonutrients that contribute to overall health and wellness.
- Consuming generous amounts of fruits and vegetables has been linked to a reduction in risk for several diseases, including stroke and heart disease, type2 diabetes and some types of cancer.

National Onion Association

The National Onion Association has a long and impressive history. It was founded in 1913 and is the official organization representing growers, shippers, brokers and commercial representatives of the U.S. onion industry. The NOA is comprised of over 600 members from the United States and abroad. The NOA is committed to educating the foodservice industry and consumers about bulb onions, their many uses and their wealth of healthy attributes.

As well as being a low-calorie food, fat, sodium and cholesterol free onions contain generous amounts of a flavonoid called quercetin. Studies have shown that quercetin protects against cataracts, cardiovascular disease and some types of cancer. Quercetin is one category of antioxidant compounds. These help delay or slow the oxidative damage to cells and tissues of the body. There are a variety of other naturally occurring chemicals known as organosulfur compounds that can be found in onions and these have been linked to lowered blood pressure and cholesterol levels.

According to the National Onion Association, onions represent the third largest fresh vegetable industry in the United States.

California Tomato Growers Association, Inc

The California Tomato Growers Association has been the voice of tomato growers for more than 50 years. It is grower owned and operated and works to ensure the stability of California's tomato growers through economic, public policy and business leadership. According to the CTGA, California tomato growers produce more than 90 percent of the nation's processed tomatoes and nearly half the world's total processed tomato tonnage. Their mission statement is: "The CTGA is an association of California processing tomato growers that provides economic, public policy and business leadership for the benefit of growers and the industry. The Association represents grower interests through services to its members including bargaining, communications and advocacy to ensure the stability, viability and prosperity of the industry."

Here are a few tomato health tips, fresh from the CTGA Web site, www.tomatogrowers.org:

- Better than one-a-day: Skip the vitamin pill and start your day with a glass of tomato juice. One (4oz) tomato supplies about one-third of the daily RDA for vitamin C plus a little beta carotene, potassium, folic acid and other B vitamins, iron and fiber.
- Fight cancer, eat a tomato: Lycopene, the ingredient that makes a tomato red, can also make you well. Lycopene is a powerful antioxidant and has been shown to prevent cancer.
- More power to the tomato: Consuming tomatoes, tomato sauce and even pizza twice a week is associated with a slightly reduced risk of prostate cancer. Other research has shown benefits against cervical, stomach and other cancers.

National Onion Association

The National Onion Association was founded in 1913 as the official organization representing growers, shippers, brokers and commercial representatives of the U.S. onion industry. According to the NOA website, www.noa.org, their organization is dedicated to "1) compiling and disseminating onion industry information, 2) increasing the visibility and consumption of onions, 3) tracking federal legislative and regulatory issues, 4) monitoring international trade and 5) conducting industry-wide educational conventions."

The NOA is also dedicated to the "foodservice industry, as well as, consumers about bulb onions and their many uses." According to the USDA, the estimated per capita consumption of onions in 2004 was 19 pounds per person. This is an increase of nearly 56 percent in the past two decades.

The USDA has again begun promoting the importance of a high intake of fruits and vegetables with the newly published MyPyramid, which shows the fruits and vegetables portion of the pyramid as one of the largest sections. Onions are low-calorie food, contain no fat, sodium or cholesterol and are a great source of dietary fiber, vitamin C, vitamin B6 and potassium.

Please visit our web site for free recipes and party planning ideas

www.vivatortilla.com